Small Practices

A Guide to
Negotiating the
Planning Maze

John Collins OBE DipArch (Birm) SPDip RIBA FRTPI
and Philip Moren BA (Hons) MRTPI

RIBA Enterprises

© John Collins and Philip Moren, 2002
Published by RIBA Enterprises Ltd, 1-3 Dufferin Street, London EC1Y 8NA

ISBN 1 85946 085 2
Product Code 21001

British Library Cataloguing in Publications Data
A catalogue record for this book is available from the British Library

Publisher: Mark Lane
Commissioning Editor: Matthew Thompson
Project Editor: Katy Banyard
Editor: Ramona Lamport
Cover Illustration: Louis Hellman
Series design by Red Hot Media
Typeset by US^{2}Design
Printed and bound by Bell & Bain

The information contained in this book is given for guidance purposes only and does not purport to be a definitive statement of planning law, policy or practice. While every effort has been made to check its accuracy, neither the authors nor the publishers can accept any responsibility for any actions based on the use of this *Guide*, and they will not be liable for any consequent damages. Readers should therefore make their own checks. The views expressed are the solely the opinions of the authors and do not reflect those of any client or employer.

Acknowledgements

We would like to thank all those people who made their individual contributions to the preparation of this book, especially:

Edward Barnes, Walker, Smith & Way; James Brotherhood, James Brotherhood Associates; Christopher Brummitt, Christopher Brummitt Architects; Anthony Burgess, Planning Portal; Dave Chetwyn, Stoke-on-Trent City Council; Murray Graham, Susan Hughes & Associates; Nick Taylor, Wigan MBC; Daniel Thompson, CABE; John Tweed, Tweed Nuttall Warburton; Tony H. Walton, Ret Architect & Town Planner; and Michael Wildblood, Wildblood Macdonald.

And, of course, Mary Webster who helped us with drawing up our flowcharts.

Last, but not least: Matthew Thompson, Ramona Lamport, Katy Banyard, Louis Hellman and all the Small Practices series editorial team at RIBA Enterprises.

About the authors

John Collins is a Past President of the Royal Town Planning Institute and Past Regional Chairman of the RIBA in the North West, and has practised at different stages of his career as an architect and as a town planner. He has worked in local government, in Birmingham, Coventry and latterly as County Planner of Cheshire. This followed a four-year spell in the private sector as an associate in an architectural and planning consultancy. He has experienced life as a civil servant both in the UK and overseas and has run his own planning consultancy, including a short period on the board of a Development Corporation. Currently he is a consultant to the Tweed Nuttall Warburton practice in Chester and represents the RTPI on the city's Conservation Area Advisory Committee.

Philip Moren is a Chartered Town Planner and practises as a Planning Consultant. He has worked for three local planning authorities, as a Consultant to FPDSavills (International Property Consultants) and as a part-time Inspector for An Bord Pleanála (the Irish Planning Appeals Board). He has extensive experience of the planning systems in England, Wales and Ireland, advising both public and private sector clients.

Other titles in the Small Practices series

A Guide to Marketing on a Shoestring
by Ian Martin

A Guide to Drawn Information
by Mervyn Hill

A Guide to Graphic Presentations
by Neil Parkyn

A Guide to Starting a Practice
by RIBA Publications

A Guide to Working with Consultants
by Neil Parkyn

A Guide to Painless Financial Management and Job Costing
by RIBA Publications

A Guide to Keeping Out of Trouble
revised and extended edition
by Owen Luder

A Guide to Managing IT
by Richard Watson and Stephen Lockley

A Guide to Sound Practice
by Stanley Cox

A Guide to Successful Client Relationships
by Sue Carmichael

Contents

Working together

To many architects, planners are the personification of Ogden Nash's Mr Henderson:

There goes Leon
Glowing like neon.
He's got an appointment
In somebody's ointment.

Town planners and architects are not always the cosiest of bedfellows.

To quote from a recent *RIBA Journal* report on Ribanet Conferencing, 'members return to a favourite subject: are planners dim, incompetent or just spineless?' And some planners are heard to ask similarly unflattering questions about architects!

The main job of this *Guide* is to help key members of the built environment professions to work together as one team. This can only be achieved when each has confidence and trust in the other's abilities, and an understanding of each other's responsibilities. This *Guide* aims to develop that understanding.

In a foreword to the *Citizen's Guide to Town and Country Planning*, first published by the Town and Country Planning Association in 1986, the late Anthony Greenwood, then Minister of Housing and Local Government wrote, 'Plans to reshape towns or to preserve the countryside, and the countless decisions on individual planning applications, are too often inadequately explained. Prejudice and misunderstanding come from lack of clear information.'

It is not only citizens, but also many architectural practitioners caught up in the planning process – *the planning maze* – who find themselves in dire need of clear information and guidance. We hope that this handbook will help to guide you through the maze.

What guidance are you looking for?

An exhaustive library of information has been published and is available (not least on the Internet), covering all aspects of the complex town and country planning system in the UK. This Small Practices *Guide* aims to provide a distillation of material of most use to architects, in a concise form. That does mean, of course, that we have had to leave much out. However, any deficiencies should be remedied by following the links to the key sources of further information included at Appendix A.

The *Guide* provides an outline of the framework of plan-making and development control in England and Wales, plus up-to-date reference sources for all practitioners involved with the planning process:

- Where to go for more information?
- How to avoid the pitfalls and keep abreast of the complex and ever-changing law and practice related to land-use and environmental planning?

- What appear, from experience, to be the most effective methods of dealing successfully with the planning bureaucracy?

Tips on using the *Guide*

This *Guide* deals mainly with planning in England, although we have tried to highlight the differences with the similar system in Wales, where appropriate. While Northern Ireland, Scotland, the Channel Islands and the Isle of Man all operate their own variations of the same theme, these are based on different legislation and are thus beyond the scope of this *Guide*. However, the planning essentials, as well as ways of dealing positively with the planning bureaucracy, is fairly universal.

While the *Guide* is not intended to act as a primary reference point on planning law, inevitably we have had to include much background material of a somewhat dry and rather legalistic nature. As far as practicable, we have tried to simplify this and have explained any unusual terms and expressions when they first appear in the *Guide*. We have not therefore included a glossary; however, a useful glossary of basic planning terms may be found on the Planning Portal website (see Appendix A).

Change is in the air

This *Guide* has been compiled at a time when the whole shooting match of planning is very much under the spotlight.

The *Citizen's Guide*, written many years ago by Denis Riley, ex-county planning officer of Staffordshire and one of the architects of the Town Development Act 1952, stated clearly that, 'the object of town and country planning is to secure better conditions for living and working, for education and recreation, for all of us, wherever we live.'

Like the little slave girl, Topsy, in *Uncle Tom's Cabin*, over the past half-century the system has 'grow'd'. It has developed and become more and more complicated. Government (as well as the business community and many members of the public) now believe that it is showing its age. In their view, it is not meeting all the objectives set out in that early *Citizens Guide*. And so in December 2001 the Government published a Green Paper for public debate, *Planning: Delivering a Fundamental Change*, proposing the biggest shake-up to the system in England since the Second World War. There are similar proposals in Wales.

The Royal Town Planning Institute (RTPI) itself has been debating a manifesto for change, entitled *New Vision for Planning*. This new vision, which the Institute's members have now adopted, is built around the core ideas of a planning that is:

- *spatial*: dealing with the unique needs and characteristics of places;
- *sustainable*: looking at the short-, medium- and long-term issues;
- *integrative*: in terms of the knowledge, objectives and actions involved;
- *inclusive*: recognising the wide range of people involved in planning.

In all these matters, the RTPI makes it clear that planning must be *value-driven*: concerned with identifying, understanding and mediating between conflicting values. It must also be *action-oriented*, driven by the twin activities of 'mediating space and making of place'.

Following wide-ranging public consultation on the Green Paper, in July 2002 the Office of the Deputy Prime Minister (ODPM) set out the Government's plans for transforming the planning system 'so that it is faster, fairer and more predictable'. Many of the proposed changes will require legislation to bring them fully into operation, and thus a new Planning and Compulsory Purchase Bill has emerged recently. Early indications are that an ambitious timetable has been set for progressing it through parliament, with the bill entering its final stages perhaps as soon as early 2003. Key proposals include replacing the existing complex hierarchy of structure and local plans with 'local development frameworks', speeding up public inquiries, introducing business planning zones, simplifying compulsory purchase procedures and, most importantly, giving to planning a clearly defined statutory purpose: a positive role, promoting sustainable development and spearheading regeneration. Strategic planning powers are also to be taken away from the counties.

Alongside these reforms, a new bill has also been introduced to pave the way for regional government in England. Eventually, this will result in a three-tiered system of planning responsibility; Government on top, followed by the regions and then a single tier of local authorities.

The most relevant, substantive changes proposed are outlined in Section 8.

So, just as we are going to print, the planning maze is on the way to having some of its fabric, its pathway, refurbished. These changes are intended to produce more opportunities for imaginative designers and developers, as well as being more responsive to the needs of local communities. While the current planning system will carry on until the new Act takes effect, local authorities have been urged to start adopting some of the new measures straight away. So there could well be some hiccups in store for the unwary!

Users of this Guide are thus advised to check on progress of both bills and any subsequent changes that may emerge. This can be done by visiting the websites of the Office of the Deputy Prime Minister and the National Assembly for Wales. You will find their addresses (URLs) on page 70, in Appendix A.

Section 1

1.1 Generally

Put simply, planning is the mechanism by which the use of land and buildings is controlled in the public interest. It does this through the preparation by local planning authorities (LPAs) of a *development plan,* and the consideration by them of planning applications against the policies and proposals in that plan, exercising their *development control* function. Together with *enforcement,* these plan-making and control functions form what has been described as the 'planning trinity'.

The development control function is the area in which architects are most likely to deal. Essentially, it is a quasi-judicial process in which 'material considerations', including economic, environmental, social and other factors, are weighed in the balance. The planner is thus piggy-in-the-middle, having to reconcile the needs and aspirations of competing interests, in order to maintain an appropriate balance between the development industry and the community at large. This involves protecting the natural and built environment, and promoting sustainable patterns of land-use and development.

1.2 Legislation

The current system is based principally on four consolidating Planning Acts, the primary legislation:

- Town and Country Planning Act 1990 (hereafter referred to as the 'main Planning Act').
- Planning (Listed Buildings and Conservation Areas Act) 1990.
- Planning (Hazardous Substances) Act 1990.
- Planning (Consequential Provisions) Act 1990.

A number of new or amended provisions were later incorporated within this legislation by the Planning and Compensation Act 1991.

In addition, there is a range of subordinate legislation in the form of statutory instruments, including a variety of development Orders, rules and regulations, which deal with matters of detail.

As we have explained in the Introduction and at Section 8, new legislation is emerging to bring about reforms to the system. However, at the time of preparing this Guide, it is not known to what extent existing statutory provisions will be superseded, saved or amended. Again, we urge users to monitor events closely.

1.3 Government advice

Both the requirements of relevant legislation and the way in which the planning system should work in practice are explained in Circulars, Planning Policy Guidance Notes, Technical Advice Notes, and in other Government pronouncements. We say more about national planning policies in Section 2.

1.4 Administration of the system

The planning system is administered by 'local planning authorities', which include:

- county councils;
- district councils;
- unitary authorities (that is, single tier councils, combining the functions of both county and district councils);
- National Park authorities;
- exceptionally, special arrangements may be made for dealing with planning applications in certain areas, such as housing action trust areas, etc.

In addition, the Secretary of State (through a number of regional Government Offices), the National Assembly for Wales and the Planning Inspectorate all play key roles in policy formulation, development plan-making and determining applications for planning permission or similar consent.

Although town, parish and community councils must be consulted or notified on certain applications, they have no decision-making powers. Their role in the planning process is therefore purely advisory.

1.5 How the development control system works

The operational principles of the planning system are explained in Planning Policy Guidance Note 1: General Policy and Principles (PPG1) issued in 1997. This makes it clear that the Government is committed to a *plan-led system* of development control. Section 54A of the main Planning Act requires that decisions made should be in accordance with the development plan, unless material considerations indicate otherwise. Thus applications which go against relevant policies in the plan should not be allowed unless there are good planning reasons to justify permission.

1.5.1 Tests for decision-makers

Generally, the test for decision-makers is whether any proposed development would cause 'demonstrable harm to interests of acknowledged importance'.

Planning terminology amongst practitioners varies, and such harm may also be described as 'material harm', or 'unacceptable' harm. However, in the case of conservation areas (as explained in Section 3), with listed buildings and certain sensitive areas, a stricter test should be applied. Here it is necessary to avoid any harm, as opposed to 'material harm'. The distinctions may appear subtle but are crucial and are not always understood, even by those responsible for operating the system.

1.5.2 Meaning of 'development plan'

The hierarchy of plans is outlined in Section 2. However, within a district, the term 'development plan' will include plans prepared at both county and district levels, such as the structure plan for the area and any local plan, but for the purposes of Section 54A these must have been statutorily *adopted* (that is, finally approved) by the relevant authorities. Elsewhere, the development plan may comprise a single all-purpose plan, such as an adopted unitary development plan. However, emerging plans may be taken into account as material considerations, and the weight to be attached to them will increase as each successive stage in their preparation is reached.

1.5.3 Material considerations

In principle, any consideration which relates to the use and development of land is capable of being a planning consideration and over the years the scope of such considerations has widened. The Courts have ruled that material considerations include the following (the list is not exhaustive):

- The development plan.
- Basic factors involved in land-use planning, such as the number, size, layout, siting, design and external appearance of buildings and the proposed means of access, together with landscaping, impact on the character and appearance of the area, existing and proposed living conditions, highway safety, ecology, archaeology, the availability of infrastructure, and other environmental considerations.
- Government statements of planning policy.
- Emerging policies, in the form of draft departmental circulars and policy guidance, depending on the context.
- The views of third parties.
- Planning gain (see 5.10).
- Availability of alternative sites.
- Public concerns about safety/perception of harm.
- Need, and national and local economic considerations.
- 'Enabling development' (that is, development which would achieve a significant benefit to a heritage asset, although it would otherwise be rejected as being contrary to planning policy – follow link to English Heritage website at Appendix A for further information).
- The ability of local planning authorities to impose conditions.
- Precedent.
- Personal hardship, in certain circumstances.
- Sustainability.
- Issues of viability, and other financial considerations, in certain circumstances.
- Certain social and cultural matters (e.g. maintenance of the Welsh language and identity).
- Existing site uses and characteristics, its planning history, and the effect of not granting permission.

1.5.4 Considerations which are not material

Matters which are not material planning considerations include those regulated by other legislation, objections on moral grounds (for example, to betting, alcohol or sex-related uses), the effect of a proposed development on property values, the maintenance of private views (unless these coincide with important public views), and the protection of other individual interests, except where these are also in the interests of the public as a whole. Legal restrictions, such as covenants, easements and rights of way, or commercial competition (in itself), are thus not relevant when considering a planning application.

1.5.5 Balancing considerations

PPG1 explains that if the development plan contains relevant policies, and there are *no* other material considerations, the application (or appeal) should be decided in accordance with the development plan. However, where there are other material considerations, the development plan should be the starting point, and the other material considerations weighed in the balance when reaching a decision. The age and relevance of the plan's policies should be considered, as they might have been overtaken by events or superseded by more recent Government planning policy guidance. Where a local planning authority proposes to grant planning permission for a development that is a significant departure from the development plan, the Secretary of State must be notified so that he can consider whether to intervene, and 'call-in' the application for his own decision.

1.5.6 Making proposed developments acceptable

When dealing with applications for planning permission/other consents, a planning authority may request amendments or improvements to the submitted proposal, impose conditions on the permission, or require the applicant to enter into a 'planning obligation' in respect of the use or development of the application site or of other land or buildings. These matters are explained under Section 5.

2.1 National planning policy

There are no national physical plans, only a series of national planning policies, issued by the Government, on a range of issues. These guide not only the preparation of development plans but also the policies within them.

In England, these are mainly expressed in the form of *Planning Policy Guidance Notes (PPGs)*. Each PPG sets out the national policy on a particular topic. For example, PPG2 deals with Green Belt policy. So far, some 25 PPGs have been published and these are listed at Appendix A.

In Wales, the framework of current land-use policies is set out mainly in 'Planning Policy Wales' March 2002, supplemented by a similar topic-based series of *Technical Advice Notes Wales (TANs)*. These are also listed at Appendix A. Some policies and procedural advice remains in the form of old Welsh Office (WO) circulars.

Current planning policies place strong emphasis on sustainable patterns of development, mixed-use development and better design. The Government is committed to delivering an 'urban renaissance', with greater re-use of previously-developed or so-called 'brownfield' land – especially for housing – and the location of development where there is good access to public transport, services and facilities. All this, it is hoped, will reduce our dependence on the car, the loss of greenfield land, and result in better living and working conditions in our towns and cities.

2.2 The European Spatial Development Perspective (ESDP) and regional plans

Do not be alarmed. The ESDP is not a grand physical plan for Europe, neither is it an attempt to harmonise the planning systems of all the countries in the Union. The EU, in its spatial approach, aims to encourage discussion between its partners, balancing competition and co-operation, leading to enhanced social as well as economic cohesion, striking a balance, and acting as a catalyst for action.

Speaking at an ESDP Forum in Brussels in February 1999, Richard Caborn, then UK environment minister, explained: 'The ESDP highlights the pulling-together of sectoral policies. We have been doing this in the UK... It reinforces developing thinking in the UK... The UK Government has proposed that Regional Planning Guidance should move towards becoming comprehensive spatial Strategies.'

A number of regional assemblies in England have now taken this on board, and have referred to the changing context of ESDP in developing their regional strategies.

2.3 Regional planning guidance (RPGs)

Regional planning guidance has been issued for each of the English regions. It is prepared on behalf of the Secretary of State by *ad hoc* teams under the control of each regional Government Office.

RPGs are planning strategies that identify a number of key issues affecting sustainable patterns of spatial development and transport patterns over the next two decades within a region. They set out the overall scale and nature of change to be accommodated, its broad location and the physical form of the development itself.

2.4 Structure plans

These are prepared by and cover counties, National Parks and most all-purpose ('unitary') councils outside the main cities. They take their lead from national and regional planning guidance, and set out key strategic policies, including the general amount and location of new housing, employment and other development. They provide the overall framework for local plans and will normally deal with a period of ten to 15 years.

Structure plans comprise a 'written statement' and a 'key diagram', illustrating the general policies.

2.5 Local plans and supplementary planning guidance

Local plans are prepared by and cover district council areas, and some unitary and National Park authorities. They set out local planning policies which work-up in detail the broad strategy of the structure plan (to which they must generally conform), to guide day-to-day planning decisions. They also identify specific sites for development. Local plans normally cover a period of about ten years.

A local plan will include a written statement, which contains the plan's policies and proposals with reasoned justification, and a 'proposals map' on an Ordnance Survey base.

Many local planning authorities prepare 'supplementary planning guidance' to expand upon local plan policies. Examples of these would be a 'planning brief' for a specific site, explaining how it should be developed, or a 'design guide' for householder developments, residential development or shopfronts, etc. These are issued for guidance only and do not form part of the statutory development plan. They are thus given less weight in the decision-making process.

2.6 Minerals and waste local plans

These are prepared by counties, National Parks and some unitary authorities. They set out policies for the control and location of mineral workings and the disposal of waste.

2.7 Unitary development plans (UDPs)

Prepared by authorities mainly in the large cities (London included), metropolitan and a few non-metropolitan unitary areas, and in Wales, UDPs combine the structure and the local plan functions. They are split into two parts. Part I contains the strategic policies, Part II sets out the detailed policies and proposals. They normally cover a period of ten years, and have a 'written statement' and 'proposals map'.

2.8 The Spatial Development Strategy for London

This is similar to a structure plan in that it sets out strategic policies, proposals and guidance for the unitary authorities in Greater London to follow when reviewing their UDPs.

2.9 The system in Wales

When local government in Wales was reorganised in 1996 with the setting up of the National Assembly for Wales, the new Welsh authorities inherited structure plans (prepared by the former county councils), and local plans (prepared in the main by the district councils and National Park authorities). Where they have been 'adopted', these still constitute the 'development plan' until superseded by UDPs now in the course of preparation.

In recognition of their special interest, qualities or role, Government agencies and local planning authorities have designated certain areas of countryside, townscape, individual buildings or other features as being worthy of particular protection. Many of these are subject to additional statutory controls and procedures. They include the following.

3.1 National Parks

These are designated by the former Countryside Commission (now known as the Countryside Agency), are subject to confirmation by the Secretary of State, and are the highest form of landscape protection. The main statutory purposes of National Parks include the conservation and enhancement of their natural beauty, wildlife and cultural heritage. The relevant National Park authorities also have a statutory duty to promote opportunities for public understanding and enjoyment of their special qualities, and to foster the economic and social wellbeing of their local communities. In the event of conflict between these different duties, priority is given to conservation. In addition to influencing the consideration of planning applications, especially for major developments, certain permitted development rights are restricted in National Parks.

3.2 Areas of Outstanding Natural Beauty (AONBs)

These are designated in much the same way as National Parks, under the same legislation, and are in effect the next step down in the national hierarchy of landscape protection. The main purpose of designation is conservation of their natural beauty and thus planning decisions will favour this. However, regard must also be had to the needs of agriculture, forestry and other uses, and to the economic and social wellbeing of the area. But, unlike National Parks, the promotion of recreation is not an objective of designation.

Permitted development rights are reduced in AONBs (see 5.1).

3.3 Green Belts

Green Belts cover about 12 per cent of England (about the same as built-up areas) and are established through development plans (structure plans dealing with the general extent, and local plans defining the boundaries). Many of England's larger towns and cities are surrounded by Green Belt. At present, there are no Green Belts in Wales, which so far has operated a broadly similar system of 'green barriers'.

Relevant guidance for England is set out in PPG2: Green Belts 1995. This explains that they have five purposes:

- To check the unrestricted sprawl of large built-up areas.
- To prevent neighbouring towns from merging into one another.
- To assist in safeguarding the countryside from encroachment.
- To preserve the setting and special character of historic towns.
- To assist urban regeneration by encouraging the recycling of derelict and other urban land.

It should be noted that Green Belts are entirely functional; their designation is not a reflection of their landscape quality. An essential characteristic of Green Belts is their openness. In the main, therefore, development within them is prohibited – there is a presumption against so-called 'inappropriate development', which should not be permitted except in 'very special circumstances'. PPG2 advises that development will be inappropriate unless it is for certain defined purposes. These include:

- agriculture and forestry (unless permitted development rights have been withdrawn);
- essential facilities for sport and outdoor recreation, for cemeteries, and for other uses of land which preserve the openness of the Green Belt and which do not conflict with the purposes of including land in it;
- limited extension, alteration or replacement of existing dwellings;
- limited infilling in existing villages (either 'washed over' or 'inset', that is, excluded from the Green Belt) and limited affordable housing for local community needs under development plan policies;
- limited infilling or redevelopment of major existing developed sites identified in adopted local plans, which meet certain criteria;
- the reuse of buildings, in certain circumstances.

An important feature of Green Belts is their permanence, although their boundaries may be reviewed periodically and altered in exceptional circumstances.

3.4 Nature conservation sites

Essentially, these may be divided into those which are Sites of Special Scientific Interest (SSSIs) or Local Nature Reserves, which are both statutory designations, and those that are non-statutory nature reserves or 'sites of importance for nature conservation', which are established by a variety of private and public bodies (including local planning authorities). All sites of national and international importance are SSSIs and are the responsibility of English Nature, who must be consulted on any planning application that would affect an SSSI.

Further information on the complex relationship between planning control and nature conservation is given in PPG9: Nature Conservation (England only) and TAN5: Nature Conservation and Planning (Wales).

3.5 Historic and archaeological interests

In addition to normal planning controls, the Planning (Listed Buildings and Conservation Areas) Act 1990 provides special controls for the protection of certain historic buildings and designated conservation areas.

3.5.1 Listed buildings

From time to time, buildings of special architectural or historic interest may be 'listed' (that is, added to a statutory list approved by the Secretary of State or National Assembly). The effect of this is to require specific consent for any demolition, or internal or external works that would affect the special interest of a listed building. This is regardless of whether any physical feature affected is mentioned in the list description, or if any planning permission is also necessary. The need for such consent may also extend to buildings or other structures attached to or within the curtilage of a listed building (that is, the area of land associated with the building). There are a number of tests as to whether an object or structure falls within a curtilage for the purposes of listed building control and these are explained in PPG15. However, listed building consent is not normally required for repairs (although these should always be discussed with the local planning authority beforehand).

Listed buildings are graded according to their relative importance:

- Grade I: buildings of exceptional interest (about two per cent).
- Grade II*: more than average special interest, but not outstanding (about four per cent). Often these will have fine interiors or strong historical associations.
- Grade II: buildings of special architectural or historic interest that warrant every effort being made to preserve them (about 94 per cent).

The statutory list (and accompanying maps) may be inspected at local planning authority offices. The National Monuments Record, the national public archive of English Heritage, provides a range of very helpful services, some of which are free (see Appendix A for website). In Wales, the equivalent body is known as CADW (Welsh Historic Monuments).

3.5.2 Conservation areas

Conservation areas are designated by local planning authorities and are 'areas of special architectural or historic interest, the character or appearance of which it is desirable to preserve or enhance.' Over 9,000 conservation areas have been designated in accordance with guidelines issued by the Government and English Heritage/CADW. The main consideration is the quality and interest of the area, rather than that of individual buildings, although conservation areas will of course often include a high proportion of listed buildings. Although there is no statutory requirement to do so, it is normal practice for planning authorities to consult residents and others affected, before making a conservation area. Increasingly, this is done as part of the local development plan-making process.

Development within conservation areas is not ruled out. However, when considering applications within a conservation area, decision-makers have a statutory duty to pay special attention to the desirability of preserving or enhancing its character or appearance. The Courts have held that this does not mean that all developments must *positively* 'preserve or enhance', merely that the character and appearance of a conservation area should not be harmed by the proposed development.

Permitted development rights are reduced within conservation areas and in some cases may be removed altogether by a so-called Article 4 Direction. There are also special controls over trees and over the display of advertisements. In addition, conservation area consent is required for most demolition works. We say more about procedures within conservation areas under Section 5.

3.5.3 Scheduled monuments and areas of archaeological importance

The Ancient Monuments and Archaeological Areas Act 1979, as amended, deals with controls over the carrying out of works to a scheduled monument and with the designation of 'areas of archaeological importance'. Where development would damage or alter a scheduled monument, it is first necessary to apply to the Secretary of State (English Heritage) for Scheduled Monument Consent. The procedure for this is similar to that for called-in planning applications, prompting a public inquiry or hearing so that interested parties can express their views. Consent may be granted, with or without conditions, or refused. A consent will lapse after five years, unless the works have been carried out or started.

Areas of archaeological importance have been designated in certain historic centres (including, for example, Chester and York). However, relevant statutory powers are intended to allow time for 'rescue archaeology', investigation and record, rather than preventing damage to archaeological interests.

Further information is set out in PPG16: Archaeology and Planning 1990 (England only).
In Wales, Welsh Office Circular 60/96: Planning and the Historic Environment: Archaeology contains similar advice.

3.6 Other heritage designations

Although *not* subject to any additional statutory controls, these include the following:

- World Heritage sites.
- Heritage Coasts.
- Historic Parks and Gardens.
- Historic Battlefields.

Further information on listed buildings, conservation areas and other heritage assets is set out in PPG15: Planning and the Historic Environment 1994 and in Wales, in WO Circular 61/96.

4.1 Grow your role!

Architect Michael Wildblood has written:

> The one area where architects excel over all others is in the conceptual design of buildings and whether we like it or not, the framework for translating these skills into increased value for our clients is to 'grow' their role in the planning process.

> I believe that if architects could increase their skills in influencing the drawing up of development plans, in relating their designs to the policies of these plans and central Government advice, and in being able to write about them as well as draw them (PPG1 design statements and public inquiry/written reps evidence), we would be a more respected profession.

So how can you 'grow your role' in the plan-making process?

The days are long gone when the first you heard that a land-use plan had even been prepared was when the local authority published it, and announced that it had been adopted! Over the years, planning authorities have experimented with ways to involve everyone whose lives would be affected by a new plan and have their say in its preparation. Thus, the involvement of individuals, communities and the whole gamut of interest groups – including industry and commerce – has been developed and written into successive Government land-use plan-making legislation. Today, no one can truthfully say that there has been no opportunity in the development policy and plan-making process when their views could be expressed and be taken into account.

4.2 Key involvement stages in plan-making

'Constant change is the steady state.' This is true for many development plans and the policies embedded in them, be they at national, regional or local level. New plans are being drawn up, while others are being reviewed or altered. Goal posts are moved. So, in your clients' interests as well as your own, you should not only keep vigilant, but also be proactive.

If any of your clients has not already commissioned a planning consultant to look after their property interests (and this is a specialist job), then as soon as the first draft proposals of any plans are published, it is vital that you study them carefully to check whether their land-use planning interests are affected. You may well find that it is proposed to change the use of land currently earmarked for one form of development to another, far less acceptable to your client. For example, when reviewing existing plans, in recent years many planning authorities have sought to remove certain existing greenfield allocations or sites which do not perform well in sustainability terms. You may also discover that it is proposed to change or tighten-up more general policies which, although not site-specific, might indirectly not be in the best interests of either yourself as a practitioner, or your current or prospective clients.

Or, of course, you may wish to influence the contents of an emerging plan to actively *promote* a particular development, or to secure more favourable policies or circumstances in advance of any application for permission.

But the process of plan-making, at whatever level, can extend over several years, with lengthy intervals between successive stages. Anyone wishing to get involved must therefore be prepared for a long haul!

4.2.1 National and regional level

There are a number of opportunities to feed in ideas and make your views known when change is in the air. At national level, you can input your ideas by responding constructively to Green Papers and the published drafts of PPGs, TANs, etc.

At regional level, you can do the same by commenting on draft RPGs. Stages at which you can do this are during the public consultation stage on:

- a 'regional issues' paper;
- the resultant 'strategy' document; and
- the draft RPG and its public examination (this is, a hearing into the main issues).

An end-date is always given for the period of consultation. Do not miss this or the opportunity to get your ideas across to Government.

4.2.2 Local level

When local authorities are preparing or reviewing structure plans, unitary development plans (UDPs) or local plans they are guided by a Government code of practice. This spells out the formal stages of plan production and where, when and how public consultation must take place.

Two separate *Guides* issued in December 1999 advise on procedures for involving the public in England in structure plans, local plans and UDPs (*Structure Plans – A Guide to Procedures*; and *Local Plans and UDPs – A Guide to Procedures*). These supplement the advice given in PPG12: Development Plans, issued at the same time.

For *structure plans*, it is explained that such opportunities will be:

- during consultation prior to the finalisation of the plan proposals;
- during the statutory six-week period for objections to the *deposited plan* proposals;
- when invited to participate in the discussion at the *Examination-in-Public (EIP)*;
- after the EIP and following the publication of the EIP panel's report, by objecting to a decision by a local planning authority not to accept a recommendation made in the report and/or changes proposed to the plan by the authority after the *EIP (modification stage)*.

In the preparation of local plans and English UDPs only, which follow a generally similar procedure, there is an additional opportunity for public involvement after the *deposit plan* stage, when a second *revised deposit* draft of the plan is published. The intention of this is to allow time for the local planning authority to try to 'negotiate away' the objections made after the plan was first placed on deposit. However, the days of the 'two-stage deposit' process are numbered, as the

Government intends to abolish this in favour of a more streamlined procedure with 'mediation' over objections to emerging plans.

In Wales, where each authority is required to produce a UDP, equivalent guidance is set out in the National Assembly's 'Unitary Development Plans – A Guide to Procedures', issued in February 2001.

So the following is a simplified guide to the main stages of the current development plan-making process, and what you should do.

4.2.2.1 Initial ideas stage (pre-deposit consultation)

Many authorities programme in a stage prior to producing the first draft of their proposals, when they ask the public for their ideas on which issues the new plan should address. This normally happens where a plan is following the single-deposit procedure. This is an important stage at which you can begin to influence emerging policies.

4.2.2.2 First deposit stage

The big opportunity you have to make your views known is as soon as the first draft of the new (or reviewed) plan is published and placed on public 'deposit' (the *deposit plan stage*). Here you can formally object to (or give your support to) any policies contained in the emerging plan which concern you, or your clients. You can also object to any matter that has not been included, but which you think should have been. Representations must be made in writing, normally on a special form, and be received by the planning authority within the prescribed period (at least six weeks). These are then considered to have been 'duly made'.

It is important to note that in order to participate in the remaining stages in the preparation of the plan, including appearing as an objector at any public inquiry, *you must have made representations at this stage.* So it is crucial that all relevant policies and proposals of the emerging plan have been evaluated thoroughly and that the correct procedures are followed.

After the period for public consultation has closed, the local planning authority will consider duly made representations and may try to resolve any objections through discussion or negotiation with the objector.

4.2.2.3 Revised or second deposit stage

In the case of local plans and English UDPs (but not structure plans), a second draft is then published (the *revised plan*). As long as you have already made formal representations at the first deposit stage, then you can again make your views known, but *only* in respect of the changes proposed. This is not a further opportunity to make new objections or to repeat the objections made at the first deposit stage. Once again, the planning authority will consider objections, try to resolve them and, where this is successful, seek their withdrawal. It may then publish its 'pre-inquiry changes', which will inform the discussion during the next stage.

4.2.2.4 The inquiry (or Examination-in-Public) and adoption stages

From here on, the process becomes embroiled in slightly differing forms of public inquiry (*Examination-in-Public* for a structure plan, *public local inquiry* for UDPs and local plans). Appearance and participation at a structure plan EIP is by invitation only. However, in the case of local plans and UDP public inquiries, objectors have the right to appear before the Planning Inspector presiding over the inquiry to explain and justify their objections, providing they were 'duly made' at the deposit stage. This may either be at a formal session, which follows a general procedure that is similar to a planning appeal public inquiry, or at a round table or informal session, which is similar to that for a hearing (see under 6.1). Alternatively, objectors may rely on existing written representations or amplify these by further, perhaps more detailed, written submissions (note that such objections carry the same weight as those made in person at the inquiry). As the inquiry is into unresolved objections, supporters of an emerging plan do not have a *right* to appear at the inquiry, but may sometimes be invited to do so in order to bolster the planning authority's case. In any event, their written representations will always be considered.

Thereafter, either the panel that presided over the EIP, or the Inspector who held the local plan public inquiry, will prepare a report for the local planning authority recommending any modifications that they consider should be made to the plan. At present, the local planning authority is not obliged to accept these recommendations but will normally do so unless there are good planning reasons (however, the Government is proposing that, in the future, Inspectors' recommendations should be made binding on the authority).

The planning authority will then publish its proposed modifications and there is a further round of public consultation (strictly limited to the modifications). Occasionally, any objections at this stage will require a further public inquiry/EIP.

Eventually, having taken into account all representations made, and having followed certain remaining procedures, the local planning authority will proceed to adopt the plan. And then, rather like the painting of the Forth Bridge, no sooner does this happen than in many cases the whole process starts all over again, with work on its review! So if you missed the boat last time, be sure to monitor progress on the next plan.

At Appendix D, we have included a simple diagram outlining the key stages in the process.

4.3 Community strategies

The Local Government Act 2000 introduced the concept of 'community strategies' as a way of *promoting or improving the economic, social and environmental wellbeing of their areas, and contributing to the achievement of sustainable development in the UK.* The duty was placed on 'principal' local authorities to each prepare its own strategy.

The Government has made it clear that 'the process by which community strategies are produced is as important as the strategy itself.' This entails setting up partnerships, which include representatives of public, private, voluntary and local community organisations. All this must result in an *action plan* and a subsequent arrangement for *monitoring* its implementation. Periodical *review* is envisaged.

Here surely is another great opportunity for members of the architectural profession to get themselves positively involved in 'growing their role'? A direct approach to your local authority to find out more on the current state of play in developing their community partnership should show you just how you could find a slot in which to get a slice of the action.

For further information, see 'Preparing Community Strategies – Government Guidance to Local Authorities', December 2000, published on the ODPM website (at www.local-regions.odpm.gov.uk under local government).

For most architects, day-to-day dealings with planning authorities will mean the submission of applications and securing permission for their proposals. It is therefore vital that they understand both the processes and the people involved.

5.1 Is permission necessary?

When considering whether permission is required, it is perhaps helpful to understand the legal definition of 'development'. Section 55 of the Town and Country Planning Act 1990 (hereafter referred to as 'the Act') defines development for which planning permission is required as:

> the carrying out of building, engineering, mining or other operations in, on, over or under land, or the making of any material change in the use of any buildings or other land.

The definition essentially has two parts: 'operational development' and 'changes of use'. For the purposes of the Act, the former includes: demolition of buildings; rebuilding; structural alterations of or additions to buildings; and 'other operations normally undertaken by a person carrying on business as a builder'. Or, as the Courts have put it, 'activities which result in some physical alteration to the land, which has some degree of permanence'. The definition of development does not extend to plant or machinery.

A change of use will not involve any physical change in the land. For it to be considered 'material' depends largely on a subjective judgment and is mainly, in the legal jargon, 'a matter of fact and degree'. Generally speaking, this will be where the new use is substantially different from the existing use, or where there has been an intensification of an existing use of such a scale that its character has changed significantly.

Section 55 of the Act excludes certain operations and uses from the definition. These include:

- maintenance, improvement or alteration works which are either internal or do not materially affect' its external appearance;
- the use of any buildings or other land within the curtilage of a dwellinghouse for any purpose incidental to the enjoyment of the dwellinghouse;
- the use of any land, or buildings on that land, for the purposes of agriculture or forestry.

In addition, various minor matters, classes of development and certain changes of use are exempted from the general need for permission, either because they are deemed not to be development for the purposes of planning control or because permission is automatically granted by a development Order or other instrument. Development by the Crown is also excluded from formal planning control.

So-called permitted development (PD) rights are set out in The Town and Country Planning (General Permitted Development) Order 1995 (GPDO), as amended, and these are explained in DoE Circular 9/95. The effect of the Order is to permit, in certain circumstances, a wide range of carefully defined developments including, for example, small house extensions and alterations, porches, garden sheds, hard surfaces, swimming pools, means of enclosure, etc. The Order also permits certain changes of use, temporary buildings and uses, caravan sites, agricultural buildings and operations, industrial and warehouse development, and other minor operations. At Appendix B, we have listed the main categories of permitted development. For an on-line 'interactive' guide to PD, visit www.planning-applications.co.uk

In certain areas, permitted development rights are more restricted. For example, within a conservation area, a National Park, an Area of Outstanding Natural Beauty or the Norfolk and Suffolk Broads, planning permission is required for certain types of development, which would not otherwise be the case. Moreover, local authorities are able to remove permitted development rights by issuing an 'Article 4 Direction', typically within a conservation area. Certain PD rights can also be withdrawn by conditions on a planning permission. In addition, PD rights may not apply where a proposed development is caught by regulations dealing with the conservation of natural habitats or environmental assessment.

The Town and Country (Use Classes) Order 1987, as amended, also provides that changes of use within broad classes are exempt from planning control. The Order is explained in DoE Circular 13/87 and a simple summary of the classes of use may be found at Appendix C.

The whole issue of what constitutes development and requires permission is somewhat complicated and is subject to extensive qualifications and restrictions. Inevitably, there is scope for wide-ranging differences in interpretation, and clarification of certain aspects has therefore frequently fallen to the Courts. In cases where the position is unclear, it is therefore prudent to discuss the matter with the local planning authority and obtain an informal written opinion. A pragmatic approach is often the best course of action. Where it is thought that something under consideration might give rise to an objection, assume the worst; it is likely that the local planning authority will argue that permission is required. In appropriate circumstances, a formal application may also be made for a 'certificate of lawfulness', as explained at 5.4.8.

When considering the need for permission, it is important to check the planning history of the site. Practices at local planning authorities vary, so it is best to telephone to establish whether prior notice of any search is required (some authorities may require up to 48 hours notice). The better equipped are able to produce a computer print-out, detailing previous planning applications. Others may rely on a card index system or a plotting sheet. In many cases, it might be necessary to inspect historical application files themselves, and this is generally permissible under 'access to information' legislation. Such files might be held on microfiche, CD-Rom, or in archive storage and these will need to be retrieved. Local authorities often charge for such a service and for providing copies of background papers. However, if there is a copy of the officer's report to committee on any history file this will usually summarise relevant issues and short-circuit the need for a full review of all the background papers.

Some planning permissions contain a condition withdrawing certain permitted development rights, thus expressly requiring permission for a particular development. The most common are conditions restricting various changes of use (typically those within Use Class Groups A and B, which relate to shops, financial services, food and drink and business uses), or those which prevent extensions and/or the insertion of windows (especially in the case of small dwellings and barn conversions). Other conditions might have been imposed to provide that any permission applies only to a named person and therefore does not run with the land (this is known as a personal permission). If such limitations have been revealed, it might be necessary to check whether these have been repeated in any planning agreement (see 5.10) entered into with the council.

Irrespective of whether planning permission is required, it might be necessary to obtain other special consents and the most common examples are explained later. In addition, building regulations approval will normally be required, and this is dealt with under separate legislation.

5.2 Who can apply?

Anyone can apply for planning permission on any land provided the application is accompanied by the relevant ownership certificate. This will confirm that the applicant is the owner, or that notice has been served on the owner (where the name and address is known to the applicant) or, in other cases, that certain steps have been taken to ascertain the name and address of any owner, including placing an advertisement in a local newspaper.

5.3 Who processes planning applications?

Most planning applications are processed by district or unitary authorities, or by the relevant National Park authority. The former include London borough councils, metropolitan and non-metropolitan councils and, in Wales, county or county borough councils. However, outside unitary authorities, certain applications (mainly involving minerals and waste disposal) are dealt with by county councils. In addition, there may be special arrangements for dealing with applications in enterprise zones, housing action trust areas, and urban development areas.

In certain circumstances, the Secretary of State (or the National Assembly for Wales) may intervene and 'call-in' an application for decision, although this happens in only a few cases where issues of more than local importance are raised.

Applications are considered by planning officers (also called development control officers). Most are Chartered Town Planners or Chartered Surveyors (Planning & Development division). Many are also architects or hold qualifications in urban design. The person who is allocated a particular application is usually referred to as the 'case officer'.

Planning officers themselves may determine certain types of application, especially for non-contentious householder or other minor developments, under so-called delegated powers (that is, clearly defined executive powers given by the councillors to their officers). More complex or controversial applications, such as those involving major developments, significant policy issues, listed buildings or objections from third parties, etc are usually decided by a committee of elected Members (normally known as the Planning and/or Development Committee, Board or Panel).

5.4 Main types of application

As architects, the main types of planning application that you are likely to come across relate to:

- outline permission;
- reserved matters approval;
- full permission;
- retrospective permission for the retention of development already carried out;
- removal or variation of conditions attached to a permission.

Other applications, stemming mainly from special controls, might also be encountered, including those for:

- listed building consent;
- conservation area consent;
- advertisement regulations consent;
- tree preservation order consent;
- hedgerow regulations consent;
- certificates of lawfulness (aka lawful development certificates – LDCs).

5.4.1 Outline permission

The main purpose of an outline application is to determine whether the principle of a proposed development is acceptable; it is however possible at this stage to seek specific approval of a detailed planning matter, or for this to be reserved as a matter for subsequent approval. The 'reserved matters' are:

- siting;
- design;
- external appearance;
- means of access;
- landscaping of the site.

It is quite common for siting or means of access to be considered at the outline stage.

Normally, an outline application will require minimal drawing work and relatively limited financial outlay for the client. Often, it will consist of little more than a site 'edged-red' on an OS Map extract and a description of the proposed development. However, local planning authorities are able, within one month of receipt of an outline application, to require the submission of further details where they consider that it ought not to be considered separately from all or any of the reserved matters. It might be necessary or desirable to support the application with an indicative layout, to demonstrate how the site could be developed. This is particularly the case where, for example, permission is sought for a specified number of units or there is doubt over whether a site could accommodate a particular proposal in a satisfactory manner.

Unless approval is sought at this stage for the means of access or siting of buildings, it is essential that any indicative layout is marked 'for illustrative purposes only', or that any submitted details are otherwise indicated as not formally forming part of the application. Otherwise, planning authorities must consider these and determine the application accordingly; the authority cannot reserve that matter by condition for subsequent approval.

Outline applications are not normally acceptable in sensitive locations, such as conservation areas, the settings of listed buildings or in Green Belts, unless extensive illustrative material is submitted, including details of elevational treatment and the relationship of the new buildings to their surroundings. Nor can they be used for changes of use.

Outline permissions are granted subject to various conditions, including those specifying time limits and requiring the subsequent approval of reserved matters. There are two types of time limit. The first requires that applications for the approval of reserved matters be made within three years. The second requires that development be started within five years of the permission or two years from the final approval of the last of the reserved matters, whichever is the longer. These limits are deemed to apply even if not stated on the 'notice of permission'. However, local planning authorities are able to specify longer or shorter time limits in appropriate circumstances and may subsequently extend these following an application to either renew the permission, or for the relevant time limit condition to be varied (in certain circumstances, even after its expiry).

Relevant regulations provide that it is possible to apply to renew an extant (that is, an existing) outline permission simply, before it lapses, by means of a letter giving sufficient information to enable the authority to identify the previous permission. In our experience, however, many local planning authorities still insist on such applications being made in the usual way.

As a general rule, such applications should be refused only where:

- there has been some material change in planning circumstances since the original permission has been granted (e.g. a change in some relevant planning policy for the area, or in relevant highway considerations, or the publication by the Government of new planning policy guidance, material to the renewal application);
- continued failure to begin the development will contribute to uncertainty about the future pattern of development in the area; or
- the application is premature because the permission still has a reasonable time to run.

It should be noted that in the case of either seeking to renew an outline permission before its expiry, or by means of an extension of time within which reserved matters should be submitted, the Courts have held that local authorities are entitled to reconsider the principle of the proposed development. They are also able to impose new conditions, not previously attached to the original permission.

The general principle is that conditions should be applied at the outline stage in the process, and that the only conditions which can be imposed when the reserved matters are approved are conditions which directly relate to those matters.

5.4.2 Reserved matters

The details of the reserved matters may be submitted for approval separately or together, or for different parts of the site. A reserved matters application must be made within the time limits and come within the scope of the outline permission; it is therefore not possible, for example, to increase the size of the site or depart substantially from its terms.

When considering an application for the approval of reserved matters, planning authorities are restricted to considering the relevant details and may not revisit the principle of the development or apply any condition that could have been reasonably foreseen at the outline stage. A good example of an acceptable condition imposed on a reserved matters approval is one that seeks to withdraw certain permitted development rights.

5.4.3 Full permission

An application for full permission requires detailed drawings to illustrate the proposed development. Clearly, both the principle of the development and the submitted details will be considered by the planning authority and further information or amendments sought as necessary. Where there is an existing outline permission, there is usually no merit in applying for full permission, instead of seeking the approval of reserved matters, unless the proposed development fails to fall within the terms of the original permission.

Such applications are generally required in the case of proposed development within conservation areas and the setting of listed buildings; and often also for certain proposals in sensitive areas where their visual impact needs to be assessed. In addition, full permission is required for householder developments, such as garages and extensions, and for changes of use and conversions, unless these are classed as permitted development.

A full planning permission normally has a life of five years and will lapse if development is not commenced within this period. However, local planning authorities are able to vary the time limits in appropriate circumstances, such as granting permission for a temporary period only, particularly in the case of certain changes of use where a trial run may be considered desirable in order to assess long-term impacts.

5.4.4 Retrospective applications

Where development has been carried out without the necessary permission, or in contravention of a condition of any permission (including those limiting the duration of a permission), Section 73A of the Act makes it possible to regularise such unauthorised development by way of a retrospective application to the local planning authority, and this will be assessed in the normal way.

5.4.5 Removal or variation of conditions

Application may also be made under Section 73 of the Act to develop land without complying with conditions attached to a previous permission. In effect, this allows for the variation or removal of planning conditions. In order to do this, the permission must still be alive; otherwise a fresh application is required. In assessing such an application, the local authority is required to consider only the conditions subject to which planning permission should be granted and, irrespective of the outcome, the original permission remains unaltered.

The relevant regulations provide that applications under Section 73 may be made by letter only, although the local planning authority is able to require the submission of further information, including drawings, if considered necessary.

5.4.6 Listed building and conservation area consent

As explained at 3.5.1, 'listed building consent' is required for works involving the demolition of all or part of a listed building and for alterations and/or extensions that would affect its character. In many instances, these works will involve development requiring planning permission. Thus an application for listed building consent will often duplicate a planning application and normally be submitted at the same time, to enable development and conservation issues to be considered together.

'Conservation area consent' is required in certain circumstances where the demolition of a non-listed building within a conservation area is proposed.

No fee is payable to the local planning authority for applications for listed building or conservation area consent, and they are processed in essentially the same way as planning applications.

Further information is set out in The Planning (Listed Buildings and Conservation Areas) Regulations 1990 (SI No 1519), PPG15: Planning and the Historic Environment, issued in 1994 and in Wales in WO Circular 61/96: Planning and the Historic Environment: Historic Buildings and Conservation Areas.

5.4.7 Advertisement regulations consent

The control of advertisements forms part of the planning system and is quite complex, especially with regard to those advertisements that are excluded from control and those falling within specified classes that benefit from deemed consent. These do not require the express consent of the planning authority, provided certain conditions are met. Because of the difficulties of applying the relevant regulations (Town and Country Planning (Control of Advertisements) Regulations), many planning authorities have a particular officer to deal with advertisement applications; similarly, the Planning Inspectorate has a specialist team of Inspectors to handle any subsequent appeals.

Unless you are satisfied that the need for consent is clear, it would be prudent to discuss this with the local authority. Generally, consent is required for the following:

- most illuminated signs;
- nearly all poster hoardings;

- fascia signs and projecting signs on shop-fronts or business premises where the top edge of the sign is more than 4.6 m above ground level;
- most advertisements on gable-ends.

The procedure for applying for advertisement regulations consent is more or less the same as that for a planning application, although a special form must be completed. The local planning authority's consideration of its merits is restricted to the two issues of 'amenity' and 'public safety'. Should consent be refused, there is a right of appeal to the Planning Inspectorate.

In England, further advice is set out in PPG19: Outdoor Advertisement Control (March 1992) and in Wales, TAN7, issued in 1997. In addition, an official explanatory booklet entitled *Outdoor Advertisements and Signs – A Guide for Advertisers* can be downloaded from the ODPM website or obtained free from the local planning authority.

5.4.8 Certificates of lawfulness

Sections 191 and 192 of the 1990 Act provide that anyone (not just a person with a legal interest in the land) may apply to the local planning authority for a 'certificate of lawfulness', more commonly known as a 'lawful development certificate' (LDC). Such a certificate is a legal document which confirms that the following is lawful:

- an *existing* operation on, or use of land, or some activity being carried out in breach of a planning condition; or
- a *proposed* operation on or use of land.

The former is referred to as a 'certificate of lawfulness of existing use or development' (CLEUD) while the latter is known as a 'certificate of lawfulness of proposed use or development' (CLOPUD).

Annex 8 of DoE Circular 10/97: Enforcing Planning Control: Legislative Provisions and Procedural Requirements explains that the development or other activity on land is lawful for planning purposes if it falls within one of the following categories and is not in breach of a planning condition or limitation:

- It does not fall within the definition of development.
- It is specifically excluded from the definition of development (such as, for example, the use of land for agriculture).
- It falls within the definition of development but is exempted from the need to apply for permission.
- It benefits from an existing planning permission.
- It is permitted development.
- It benefits from deemed planning permission by virtue of compliance with the requirements of an effective enforcement notice.
- It took place before 1 July 1948.
- It is development by or on behalf of the Crown.
- The time for taking enforcement action has expired.

As far as the last bullet point is concerned, the time limits are four years in the case of operational development and for any change of use to a single dwellinghouse, and ten years for all other changes of use.

The effect of the grant of a CLEUD is to make the specified development immune from enforcement action, provided that it is not already in breach of an existing enforcement notice. Essentially, a CLEUD is equivalent to the grant of permission. It will be precisely defined by the planning authority, with specific reference to the area of land to which the certificate relates, and will be conclusive.

Applications for CLEUDS are considered solely on the weight of the supporting documentary evidence, applying the test of 'the balance of probability'. Basically, this means that it is more likely than not that the claim is true, and is less strict than the criminal test of 'beyond reasonable doubt'. The planning merits of the development are therefore not relevant to the local planning authority's consideration. As the onus of proof is firmly on the applicant and only legal issues are involved, solicitors often handle such applications, or at least have a hand in the preparation of evidence. That evidence might include, for example, affidavits, statutory declarations, accounts, rating records, receipts, vehicle registration documents and gas/electricity bills and so forth.

As the planning authority is not able to impose any conditions when granting a LDC, a CLEUD is likely to be of greater benefit to an applicant than the possible alternative of retrospective permission. However, the planning authority is able to issue a certificate of a different description from that applied for, in order to define precisely and unambiguously what has been substantiated by the submitted evidence.

The effect of a CLOPUD is not the equivalent of a grant of permission for a proposed development, merely that unless there has been some material change in circumstances since the application date specified in the certificate, it would be lawful to proceed with the proposed development. Such a change might include, for example, the curtailment of permitted development rights through an Article 4 Direction or the designation of a conservation area.

There is a right of appeal to the Planning Inspectorate against a planning authority's refusal to grant a lawful development certificate.

5.4.9 Trees and hedgerows

Trees and hedgerows can be protected in several ways and thus consent may be required for their felling, lopping or for other surgical works.

Section 198 of the Town and Country Planning Act 1990 enables local authorities to make a Tree Preservation Order (TPO) in respect of individual trees, groups of trees or areas of woodland, where this is expedient in the interests of amenity. Such Orders must be made in accordance with the procedures set out in the Town and Country Planning (Trees) Regulations 1999 and, although objections may be lodged to proposed Orders, there is no right of appeal against their subsequent confirmation by the local authority. However, in certain circumstances it may be possible to challenge the Order in the High Court, on a point of law. Otherwise, appeals may be made only where a local authority has subsequently refused to grant TPO consent.

The effect of a TPO is to require the consent of the local authority for the 'cutting down, topping, lopping, uprooting, wilful damage, or wilful destruction' of any tree the subject of such an Order. In addition, in certain circumstances landowners are placed under a duty to replace protected trees that have been removed. TPO provisions do not apply to trees which are dying or dead, or have become dangerous, where it may be necessary for the prevention or abatement of a nuisance, or where exemptions are conferred by other relevant legislation.

Where works to a protected tree are required for the purposes of carrying out authorised development, the provisions of the TPO no longer apply. Thus a planning permission will override such protection.

Further information on tree preservation may be found in the Town and Country Planning (Trees) Regulations 1999 (England and Wales) and in two *Guides*, both published on the ODPM website, *Tree Preservation Orders: A Guide to the Law and Good Practice* (April 2000), and *Protected Trees – A Guide to Tree Preservation Procedures* (May 2000). In Wales, reference should also be made to TAN10: Tree Preservation Orders 1997.

Trees within a designated conservation area enjoy a similar level of protection to those subject to a TPO, subject to certain exceptions and procedural differences. These include a general requirement to give the local planning authority six weeks notice of any intention to fell, lop, top or otherwise damage a tree. The authority may either consent to the proposed works or make a Tree Preservation Order. If it does neither within this period, then this can be used in defence of the carrying out of such works, provided that these are done within two years. Trees under a prescribed size or species, and certain acts, may be exempted under the relevant regulations. It should be noted that more onerous replanting obligations apply than with the Tree Preservation Order regime.

Frequently, when granting planning permission, local authorities will seek to retain or protect important trees by imposing appropriate conditions. However, Government advice is that the long-term protection of trees should be secured by tree preservation orders, rather than by condition.

Under the Hedgerows Regulations 1997, it is unlawful to remove most countryside hedges without first obtaining the permission of the local authority. Any hedgerow within the curtilage of a dwelling is excluded. A leaflet, *The Hedgerows Regulations: Your Question Answered*, provides a brief summary of the law, while more detailed guidance is in *The Hedgerows Regulations 1997: A Guide to the Law and Good Practice* (available from ODPM Publication Sales Centre).

5.5 Preparing and submitting planning applications

It is perhaps self-evident that the key to a successful planning application will often lie in its careful preparation and presentation. However, all too frequently applications are not accepted, because they are inadequate, or their processing may subsequently be delayed, or they may ultimately be refused because of some failure to take into account a matter that should have been reasonably clear at the outset.

In the revised and extended edition of his RIBA Publications Small Practices series, *A Guide to Keeping out of Trouble*, Owen Luder points out that most clients are not fully aware of the problems and delays with obtaining planning approvals. In his section dealing with Town Planning Applications (page 8) he advises, 'Do not encourage over-optimism as to what will be approved and how long it will take.' He follows this with some further sound, detailed advice on keeping clients fully up to speed with the progress of their application and the tactics to follow when strong local opposition is foreseen.

Some applicants underestimate the sheer complexity of the planning process and look upon it as something of an unwelcome formality. Recognising that this is not the case, and embracing it as a 'development partner', will help greatly in ensuring that potential problems are anticipated and that emerging projects succeed. In addition, the increasing need for specialist advice of one sort or another – to address the diverse issues that are often thrown up – should always be borne in mind.

To adapt a well-known military truism: Perfect Preparation and Partnership Prevents Poor Performance in Planning!

5.5.1 Pre-application discussions

Before submitting a planning application, particularly for complex or larger developments, you should discuss the proposal with an officer of the local planning authority. You should seek clarification of the issues that might need to be addressed, the information that will need to be submitted with the application (including any impact statement), and its chances of success. If possible, get the planning authority's informal opinions confirmed in writing. This will help to avoid unnecessary delays in processing the application and ensure that possible pitfalls are identified early on. Some authorities have their own special procedures for this and are more co-operative than others, although much depends on the nature of the proposal, current workloads, and the availability of staff.

However, while it is wise to seek such advice, it should be understood that it is given in good faith, without prejudice to the formal consideration of any planning application by the local authority. Try to speak to the planning officer who is familiar with the area and would eventually deal with the application, when submitted. If you can, or it is particularly important (for example where it is necessary to inspect inaccessible buildings or for judgements to be made on matters of 'visual amenity', etc), arrange to meet on site.

Informal approaches of the planning authority are likely to be more productive if some basic preparation is undertaken beforehand, not least because it will mean that you are already aware of relevant issues and will have a much better idea of those that could require particular attention. You will also know which questions you should ask, and have time to consider how you might best respond to any questions that are likely to be put to you. This is particularly the case if the proposal is likely to be controversial. If possible, therefore, you should always try to:

- Investigate the planning history of the site, as explained at 5.1, and consider anything that might be relevant to the proposal.
- Check the adopted and/or emerging local plan/UDP designation of the site and any policies relevant to the proposal.
- In the case of larger sites, check whether a 'planning brief' has been prepared.
- Familiarise yourself with the relevant development control and highway standards adopted by the council. These will normally be set out in the local plan or UDP, in a locally adopted design guide, or in other supplementary planning guidance notes. The most common standards include those relating to access, roads and parking, public and private amenity space provision, maintenance of residential amenity (overlooking, overshadowing, etc) and affordable housing.
- Make sure that you look at the site. Assess for yourself its characteristics, constraints/opportunities, and its setting and general surroundings. If necessary, arrange for a preliminary survey, to include the location and condition of any trees on site, and changes of level.
- Prepare a simple preliminary sketch to show the form of the proposed development and send this to the relevant planning officer, in advance of the meeting. This will enable him/her to consider its merits informally and, if necessary, seek the views of more senior officers and those of colleagues in other departments.
- Check whether the planning authority has published its own planning handbook, has information sheets/leaflets available or, as is now quite common, has posted guidance notes on its website. These may explain its particular requirements, the structure of the planning department, the council's decision-making procedures, and set out other useful information.
- Find out how long it is likely to take any application to be processed, dates of relevant planning committee meetings and the extent of any delegated powers (see 5.6). Always allow sufficient time to obtain permission before development is due to start and do not simply assume that your application is one that can be determined quickly, or that permission will be automatically granted.

Where a controversial development is proposed, it is vital to secure grassroots or other third party support. It is therefore important to engage the local community and others at the outset, and carry out some form of informal consultation exercise. This might include discussing your ideas with the parish or community council, local councillors, residents groups, or those who are likely to be consulted on the application. If the proposed development involves a new or altered access, new roads or traffic generation issues, you should discuss the matter informally with the Highway Authority as many proposals which are otherwise acceptable in planning terms, may fail on highways grounds. Similarly, if the proposal includes works to a listed building or there are protected trees on site, etc separate discussions with the council's conservation officer or landscape division might also be helpful.

5.5.2 Preparing the application

Following consultation with the RTPI and others, in 2001 the RIBA issued guidance to members on *Recommended Design Stages and Procedures in the Preparation of Full Planning Applications.* This recommends that ten stages should be followed:

1. The full project brief and the functional requirements of the development should be established.

2. The physical dimensions, the condition, character and constraints of the site should be surveyed and appraised.

3. National and local government planning policy for the development of the site should be identified. Clarification should be sought and discussed with relevant authorities if appropriate.

4. If appropriate, the technological, energy and sustainability requirements for the development should be established.

5. The site should be considered and analysed in relation to its immediate surroundings and its wider urban and/or landscape setting. This does not of necessity mean that new development should be equal in design, form, mass or height with its surroundings.

6. The impact of the brief and function in relation to the site, setting, local and national policies, the relevant community or communities and the immediate and wider environment should be considered.

7. Where appropriate, investigations or consultations should be undertaken with affected interests, authorities or communities.

8. Clear and demonstrable design principles or a design vision should be established. These principles or this vision should be compatible with the criteria and interests established above.

9. A design should be prepared that is consistent throughout with the design principles or vision. The design should include consideration of space, mass, volume, plan, materials and the composition of elements.

10. The application should sufficiently illustrate the design and its expression of the design principles or design vision and the wider impact of the development. Consideration should be given to the scope and the presentation, which may need to include special drawings, diagrams, models or any other descriptive media.

The guidance note also makes clear that:

- Adherence to these procedures will not create a good design – a good design can only be created by a good designer.
- The standards are intended to indicate the considerations that will underlie most good designs. They are also applicable to listed buildings and conservation areas.
- The level of input for each item, stage or point will vary considerably according to the scale or type of development.
- Some procedures go beyond the RIBA recommended work stages for the preparation of an application for full development control approval. Other professionals or experts may be responsible for some items or tasks.

5.5.3 Drawings, documents and forms

While the specific requirements of planning authorities vary slightly, the following checklist (adapted from the DETR/CABE publication *By Design*, May 2000) sets out the drawings that will typically need to be submitted as part of an application for full permission, in order that the design can be properly assessed by planners, councillors, residents, amenity groups and others (N.B. all drawings must be in metric).

Location plan
- Scale, 1:1250 preferably, and no smaller than 1:2500.
- North point, date and number.
- Outline application property in red, and indicate adjoining property owned or controlled by applicant in blue.
- Show the application property in relation to all adjoining properties and the immediate surrounding area, including roads.
- Show vehicular access to a public highway if the site does not adjoin a road.

Details of existing site layout
- Scale, typically 1:200 or 1:500.
- North point, date and number on plans.
- Show the whole property, including all buildings, gardens, open spaces and car parking.
- Tree survey and ground levels, where appropriate.

Details of proposed site layout
- Scale, typically 1:200 or 1:500.
- North point, date and number on plans.
- Show the siting of any new building or extension, vehicular/pedestrian access, changes in levels, landscape proposals, including trees to be removed, new planting, new or altered boundary walls and fences, and new hard surfaced open spaces.
- Show proposals in the context of adjacent buildings.

Demolitions
- Any proposed demolition should be clearly shown on the plan and elevation drawings.

Floor plans
- Scale, 1:100 (1:50 often required for listed buildings).
- North point.
- In the case of an extension, show the floor layout of the existing building to indicate the relationship between the two, clearly indicating new work.
- Show floor plans in the context of adjacent buildings, where appropriate.
- For alterations to listed properties include a separate existing floor plan drawn to the same scale and an original floor plan where applicable.
- In the case of minor applications, it may be appropriate to combine the layout and floor plan (unless any demolition is involved).
- Include a roof plan where necessary to show a complex roof or alteration to one.

Elevations
- Scale, 1:50 or 1:100 (consistent with floor plans).
- Show all elevations of a new building or extension.
- For an extension or alteration, clearly distinguish existing and proposed elevations.
- Include details of materials and external appearance.
- Show elevations in the context of adjacent buildings, where appropriate.
- For shop fronts, include the entire front elevation to show the relationship with the rest of the building.

Cross sections
- Scale, 1:50 or 1:100 (consistent with floor plans).
- Provide these if appropriate.

Appendix A of PPG1: Planning Policy and Principles advises that applicants for planning permission should, as a minimum, provide a short written statement setting out the design principles adopted. This should explain the design principles and design concept of the proposed development, and how it relates to its wider context, using illustrative material where appropriate. Ideally, it should be included in a comprehensive planning report, such as that normally prepared by a planning consultant, explaining and justifying the proposal within the context of relevant national and development plan policies, stressing the benefits of the development, and arguing the case for permission. Such a report can often be key in influencing a successful outcome. If the application has been the subject of pre-application consultations, these should be mentioned and any resultant changes outlined.

Large-scale or complex applications may require other supporting material, for example, retail, environmental, transport or other assessments, including in some cases evidence that a 'sequential approach' to site-selection has been taken (that is, examining it and alternative sites against certain sustainability criteria). The need for these will usually be made clear in pre-application discussions. Certain types of development which are likely to have significant effects on the environment because of their nature, size or location must be accompanied by a formal 'environmental impact assessment', prepared in accordance with the Town and Country Planning (Environmental Impact Assessment) (England and Wales) Regulations 1999. For further information, see under 'Guidance and Advice' section on ODPM website (address at Appendix A).

Only use the application forms issued by the relevant local planning authority and do not try, for example, to amend another authority's form; otherwise your application may be returned. Think carefully about the description of the proposed development as any permission will relate specifically to this (and may have VAT implications!). If necessary, describe the development more fully in the covering letter. Make sure that the relevant ownership certificate has been completed. And do not forget to keep a photocopy of the application form, as this may be needed for any subsequent appeal.

Applications involving industry, warehousing, offices, shopping, farm buildings, farm dwellings, waste disposal and mineral extraction will normally require a separate form to be completed. Many authorities also use a simplified form for householder applications.

Generally, five copies of the application will need to be submitted to the planning authority (fewer in the case of an application for listed building consent). If the application is supported by other material, such as impact studies, etc it is advisable to provide additional copies of these, as this will assist consultation with others and avoid unnecessary delays. Always ask that one set is placed with the public copy of the application and that the contents of any written material are reported to Members of the committee who will consider the application.

Except in certain circumstances, a planning application must be accompanied by a fee, which is payable to the planning authority and is non-refundable. The relevant fees are set out in the Town and Country Planning (Fees for Applications and Deemed Applications) Regulations (see ODPM/National Assembly for Wales websites for details; the addresses are at Appendix A).

5.6 What happens to your application and what you should do

Once an application has been received it is checked to see whether it is complete (that is, valid) and a letter of acknowledgement is sent to the applicant (however, this does not necessarily confirm that the application is valid). Sometimes the planning authority will amend the description of the proposed development to ensure that it accurately reflects what is shown on the submitted drawings. So this should be checked and any concerns taken up immediately with the case officer identified in the letter as dealing with the application. The acknowledgement letter will also give a reference number (which should always be quoted in correspondence) and the date within which the planning authority intends to make a decision (eight weeks from receipt of the application, this being the statutory period following which an appeal for non-determination is possible, unless this is extended by written agreement).

Invalid applications may be returned, or retained with a request for specified deficiencies to be rectified. Typical problems include inadequate drawings, failing to complete the relevant ownership certificate correctly, or submitting the wrong fee. Remember that the planning authority will not start to consider the application until it is valid, so it is vital to ensure that all the necessary documentation is in order.

Once valid, the application will be registered (that is, entered on the public planning register), and recorded in the planning authority's computer system. The respective copies of the application are separated and one is made up into a working file which is then allocated to the case officer, normally with details of any previous planning history on the site. One copy is made available for public inspection at the reception desk. The remaining copies will be used for other consultation purposes.

As soon as possible, the case officer will arrange for the application to be advertised in a local newspaper, as appropriate, for neighbouring occupiers to be notified by letter, and/or for a notice to be displayed on site. Practice on publicising applications varies, but minimum requirements are set out in the General Development Procedure Order 1995. The planning authority has a duty to take into account all representations received, before determining the application. A period of 21 days is normally given for comments (14 days where advertised), although the planning authority is not precluded from considering comments made after this time has expired.

Special provisions apply for publicising major developments, applications affecting conservation areas and listed buildings, and for notifying the Secretary of State of 'departure applications' (that is, those conflicting with the development plan) and certain other proposals. According to the type and scale of the proposed development, planning authorities are required to consult certain persons or bodies, such as the Highway Authority, Environment Agency, local parish or community council, and various Government authorities/agencies, or other organisations and third parties. Internally, the planning authority might well consult its colleagues in other departments, such as in environmental protection, drainage, or leisure services, etc.

The planning officer will assess the application against relevant development plan policies and any other considerations and invariably carry out an inspection of the site (although there is no statutory obligation to do this). Further information on the application may be requested or amendments sought. In any event, it is always prudent to monitor progress on the application closely and to speak to the planning officer about four to five weeks after it has been submitted, as by this time he or she should have an idea of any issues that might need to be addressed, and whether the application is one that will need to be reported to committee or decided under delegated powers. Such powers vary widely and will be set out in the council's constitution, which can be inspected where required.

In response to any negotiations with relevant officers, it might be necessary to submit revised drawings. These will normally trigger a further but shorter period of public consultation (usually 14 days). We say more about negotiations at 5.7.

Once the relevant consultation periods have expired and comments have been considered, and the planning officer is satisfied that it is appropriate to do so, he or she may then determine the application under delegated powers or, if the application falls outside the scope of such powers, prepare a written report and recommendation for consideration by council Members. The extent of his or her workload and relevant performance targets inevitably will also have a bearing on when the application may be decided, and the former is probably the most common reason for delay.

Reports are usually prepared about two weeks before the date of the committee meeting. As this often acts as an informal deadline for submitting any outstanding details or information, such material should be provided well in advance, otherwise the planning officer may decide to hold the application in abeyance until the next meeting. The planning officer's report may be the subject of internal consultation and need to be cleared by more senior officers in the management hierarchy.

It is vital to try to establish when and how an application is to be decided as, according to how well things have been going, this will affect possible courses of action. For example, if it is clear that the planning officer is opposed to the application and is likely to refuse it under delegated powers, you might wish to consider asking a Member to intervene and request that the application be reported to committee, if this is possible. Among other things, this would enable relevant Members to be lobbied or, where such opportunities exist, to address the committee in person.

Planning reports to the relevant committee, which will usually sit every three to four weeks or so, should be open and impartial. Most follow the same format and, where appropriate, include a summary of:

- the proposed development and any related background information;
- the site and its surroundings;
- relevant planning history;
- relevant development plan provisions;
- consultations carried out, comments received, and views expressed in letters of objection or support, details of any petition, etc;
- the main issues and planning consideration;
- a recommendation to grant or refuse;
- draft conditions to be imposed, with reasons (however, these may be abbreviated using the planning authority's own particular code);
- the terms of any planning agreement to be sought;
- draft reasons for refusal.

In accordance with the access to information legislation, the officer's report to committee and related background papers (that is, the planning application file), must be made available for public inspection at least three clear working days before the date of the committee meeting. Many authorities exceed the minimum requirements. It is always advisable to obtain a copy of the report as soon as it is available and this is usually possible by speaking to the relevant committee clerk or the Member services department. Some authorities will fax or e-mail the report.

The benefits of getting hold of the officer's report are that:

- It enables you to check the planning officer's advice and recommendation, to confirm that any negotiations have succeeded and that any informal assurances given by the planning authority have been fulfilled. Make sure that relevant matters have been understood and are adequately summarised, nothing important has been omitted and that the report is not misleading. In some instances, a case officer's own views might have been overruled or modified in some way by more senior officers. However, while this is quite legitimate, it is normal practice to notify the applicant beforehand of any significant change, to avoid any nasty surprises.
- It will reveal the nature and extent of any local opposition or objections raised by any major third parties, if these have not already been disclosed.
- As Members will now be aware of the planning officer's advice they are better briefed and thus often more willing to discuss the application, although many will not express a view for fear of prejudicing consideration of the application at the committee meeting.
- This is when lobbying by interested parties steps up a gear and is likely to be most effective.
- It enables last minute action/negotiations to resolve outstanding issues, rectify mistakes and possibly avoid a refusal.
- Conditions, the requirements of any planning obligation, and any reasons for refusal can be considered.

If the application is recommended for refusal, your choices are:

- Let the application run and perhaps lobby councillors in the hope that they will overturn the recommendation.
- Withdraw the application, to avoid 'negative history', and perhaps consider preparing a revised proposal.
- Ask for the application to be deferred to enable further negotiations to take place. Most planning authorities will only agree to this if there is some clear evidence of an intention to overcome relevant objections, or if revised drawings have been received by the planning authority too late for them to be considered properly.

Knowing whether, when best, or how much to lobby Members during the application process can be quite hard to judge. Too much lobbying can put off decision-makers, whilst none might mean that a valuable opportunity is missed to stress the benefits of a proposed development, and too little may of course prove ineffective! Lobbying can include letters addressed to individual councillors (but beware, this may antagonise the planning officer), or speaking directly with key Members, such as the Ward Member, Chair and Vice-Chair of the planning committee, etc. Often it is more successful when conducted by the applicant, as it may be thought to be more heartfelt than when coming from an agent 'simply going through the motions'. However, large-scale or complex proposals may well require advice from a planning consultant or specialist public relations consultant.

At worst, allowing an application to run and be considered by Members will preserve the right of appeal, which is lost once an application is withdrawn. In any event, a revised application can be submitted within 12 months and this will not require a new fee provided the proposed development is of the same character or description as that the subject of the original application, and that it is submitted by the same applicant.

Many planning authorities have introduced procedures for public speaking at committee meetings, following prior notification, but this is generally limited to about three minutes per speaker. Nevertheless, this might be long enough to stress the main benefits of the proposed development and/or respond briefly to comments made by objectors. But it is doubtful in the majority of cases whether such action is pivotal in changing the outcome of the application. Regardless of whether any public speaking rights exist, it is usually a good idea to attend the committee meeting to listen to any discussion, as that might explain relevant issues and could inform any re-submission or appeal that might be lodged.

In addition to considering the planning officer's written report, at the meeting of the planning committee Members may receive an oral presentation from key officers, often aided by visual material such as slides and plans, etc and this will be supplemented by any late information received since the report was prepared. According to Member interest and how complex or controversial an application is, decisions will either be made 'on the nod' (that is, in accordance with the officer's recommendation but with no discussion of the application) or after some discussion and a subsequent vote.

Members are not bound to follow the advice of their professional advisors, but must be able to demonstrate good reasons based on land-use planning grounds for not doing so, or else will be liable for an award of costs on appeal. Typically, less than ten per cent of recommendations are overturned. In some cases, the committee might defer making a decision in order to request further information or amendments from the applicant, advice from its officers, or more consultations to be carried out. Alternatively, it might wish to look at the site itself before making a decision, or to instruct a sub-committee to do this on its behalf and report back to its next meeting with a recommendation. In such circumstances, it is common to invite interested parties to be present and there may be opportunities for speaking for or against the proposal.

Decisions made on certain applications, particularly those involving significant policy issues, may need to be referred to other committees/boards of the council, or to a meeting of the full council itself.

Following its consideration of an application, generally the committee will resolve to do one of the following things:

- grant unconditional permission/approval/consent;
- grant permission/approval/consent with conditions;
- grant permission following the prior completion of a planning obligation;
- refuse permission;
- defer a decision on the application.

At Appendix E is a simplified flowchart of what happens to an application after it has been submitted to the local planning authority.

5.7 Negotiations and tactics

According to the scale and complexity of the proposed development, at some stage in the planning process it is likely that negotiations will be necessary to address matters of concern or, where necessary, to try to overcome objections raised by either the planning authority or other interested parties. Clearly, successful negotiations often depend on the skill and experience of those involved. The following are some tips:

- Make sure that you negotiate with the right people. Identify the key players in the process, both within the authority (which are likely to include officers from various departments) and outside (e.g. Highway Authority, Environment Agency, etc). For bigger schemes, many local authorities now provide a development team approach, with a single point of contact. Unless the proposed development is one that is likely to raise significant or district-wide issues, it will rarely be necessary to start at the top (although bigger schemes are likely to be handled by more senior officers, in any event). However, where appropriate, a quick phone call to the council's development control manager will establish who is likely to deal with relevant matters. Most development control officers work in teams dealing with particular geographical areas.
- Find out something about the political composition of the council, which group holds power, what the major drivers are (e.g. economic regeneration, maintenance of the Green Belt,

affordable housing provision, etc). Does the planning authority operate within a corporate culture where development is positively encouraged, managed or generally resisted? Establish who are the key councillors that you might wish to speak with, including the relevant committee Chair and Ward Members. Beware of over-lobbying as this can be counter-productive!

- Lobbying MPs or Government departments is rarely effective.
- Establish who is likely to object to the proposed development, such as local amenity groups, etc and whether there is anything that can be done to reduce/overcome any opposition.
- Confrontation sometimes has its place in the planning process. However, a partnership approach, developing good working relationships and seeking to understand the needs and aspirations of the authority and others – and involving them in the project – is more likely to be effective. Above all, be realistic in your expectations!
- Neither planning officers nor elected Members respond well to threats, including suggestions that any refusal will be appealed, etc.
- Aggressive tactics such as 'twin-tracking' (that is, submitting identical applications simultaneously with the objective of lodging an appeal for non-determination of one, whilst continuing to negotiate on the other) can waste local authority resources and cause confusion. They are often unnecessary and ineffective (and are proposed to be outlawed by the Government; see 8.2). Similarly, submitting an application which you know to be 'overdevelopment' (because, for example, it includes too many housing units, etc), simply because you are trying to maximise the development potential of the site but are expecting during the course of negotiations to reduce its scale (and in so doing wish to appear to have made significant concessions), can be counter-productive. Rather than negotiating, planning authorities will often refuse blatantly unacceptable applications quickly, especially if any matters flagged-up during any pre-application discussions have been ignored.
- Stress any benefits of the development. Where a proposed development is likely to be acceptable in any event, it will be seldom necessary to consider any 'planning gain'. However, where a proposed development is likely to be regarded as contrary to policy, it is essential to demonstrate 'other considerations' sufficient to override such objections.
- Consider the use of other consultants and specialists. Local authorities often respond more positively in planner-to-planner negotiations, especially where there is already a good working relationship. In addition, planning officers will normally discuss matters more openly and freely where the client is not directly involved in negotiations.
- Two powerful negotiating tools that development control officers have at their disposal are bluff and delay. Knowing when planning officers are seeking to achieve their objectives by making unreasonable demands or merely expressing personal preferences requires experience and a detailed knowledge of the council's policies and national planning guidelines. However, acceding to some requests for changes to a scheme or for a planning obligation may often be better, on balance, than suffering the financial consequences of a significant delay in achieving permission.
- Before meetings with the planning authority make sure that you and any other participants are well briefed. Establish beforehand matters that are 'negotiable' and might be conceded, and those that cannot. At the end of any discussions, be clear as to what has been agreed and points for action.
- Do not rely solely on discussions. Make sure that notes of meetings are kept and that the planning authority receives subsequent correspondence detailing what has been agreed.

Remember that others may look at the application file or background papers, particularly in the event of an appeal or any challenge.

- Check the wording of emerging conditions and the terms of any obligations and, where necessary, engage the services of specialists to do this.

5.8 Decision notices

The Courts have ruled that the date of a decision is when the relevant notice is issued, and not when any committee has resolved to either grant or refuse permission. As it will often take planning authorities up to about two weeks, after the resolution, to issue a notice, if time is of the essence it may well pay to chase them up for this.

Decision notices must state clearly and precisely their full reasons for refusing permission or for any condition imposed; most planning authorities use standard reasons for refusal and/or conditions to deal with regularly encountered issues. Any relevant planning policies relied upon should also be identified in the notice.

Some planning authorities will attach a list of 'informatives' to the decision notice. These do not form part of the decision itself, but are notes setting out guidance on related matters such as the need for other statutory consents or, in the case of a refusal, some indication of the kind of development the planning authority would find acceptable.

5.9 Planning conditions

It is essential to consider carefully any conditions attached to a permission as, unless appealed, they will be deemed to have been accepted and may be enforced by the planning authority by means of a 'breach of condition notice', against which there is no right of appeal (see also under Section 7).

The general approach to conditions is that they should be imposed only where there is a clear land-use planning justification. PPG1 explains that the key test on whether a particular condition is necessary is if planning permission would have to be refused if the condition were not imposed. Detailed advice on conditions is set out in DoE Circular 11/95: The Use of Conditions in Planning Permissions. Among other things, this explains that conditions should only be imposed where they satisfy all of the following tests, and are:

- necessary;
- relevant to planning;
- relevant to the development to be permitted;
- enforceable;
- precise;
- reasonable in all other respects.

These are examined in the Circular, and examples are given of conditions which are acceptable and those that are not. Conditions can be imposed to deal with matters such as access, parking, landscaping, noise, restrictions on hours of use, etc.

Generally, conditions should only be imposed on land under the control of the applicant, whether within or outside the site, although it is possible to impose a 'negative' or *Grampian* condition (so-called after the Court case where such an approach was held to be acceptable). This prevents the commencement of development until a specified action (such as a road improvement, for example) has taken place. However, such conditions should only be imposed where there is a reasonable prospect that the specified action will happen during the lifetime of the permission.

Notwithstanding the principle that planning controls are not normally concerned with the identity of the user and that planning permission runs with the land, in exceptional circumstances conditions may be imposed to make a permission personal to the applicant. This sometimes happens where, for example, a particular business use is considered of special importance to the local economy, but in any other circumstances would be considered unacceptable. In addition, conditions may be imposed to restrict the occupation of a building, for example in the case of agricultural dwellings or staff accommodation.

Government advice to planning authorities is that generally conditions should be used in preference to planning obligations.

5.10 Planning obligations and planning gain

The term 'planning obligation' (often referred to as a 'section 106 agreement') comprises both planning agreements and unilateral undertakings. It is a deed which is legally binding on subsequent owners. It is usually created by agreement with the local planning authority. However, it may also be offered unilaterally by a developer, particularly on appeal when a developer considers that unreasonable demands are being made by the planning authority. The obligation may be positive, requiring something to be done, or negative, preventing something from happening. They may thus:

- restrict development or the use of land in a particular way;
- require operations or activities to be carried out in, on, under or over land;
- require the land to be used in a specified way; or
- require financial contributions to be made to the authority.

Like conditions, planning obligations may be used to enable development, which might otherwise be refused, to go ahead. They must, however, only be sought where they meet the following tests, and are:

- necessary;
- relevant to planning;
- directly related to the proposed development;
- fairly and reasonably related in scale and kind to the proposed development;
- reasonable in all other respects.

Anyone with an interest in the land may enter into an obligation, which will only take effect once the planning permission is granted and implemented.

In the main, obligations are used to ensure that developers provide, pay for or contribute to new or improved infrastructure and community facilities, which would not have been necessary but for their development. Some examples include: access/highways/transport arrangements; car parking, public open space, social, educational, recreational, sporting or other community provision, provided that the need for these arises directly from development, or is required to offset or replace the loss of existing resources/facilities on the site.

Obligations are sometimes used to restrict the occupancy of land and buildings (e.g. to agricultural workers or those of retirement age, in the case of sheltered housing schemes, etc), give up existing use rights or planning permissions, or to ensure the provision of affordable housing.

Government advice is that conditions imposed on a planning permission should not be repeated in a planning obligation (as this frustrates a developers right to appeal), although many planning authorities will often try to do this. When dealing with planning agreements, it is essential to seek advice from a planning solicitor or planning consultant.

Where a planning obligation no longer serves any land-use planning objective it may, on application to the planning authority, be discharged by agreement between the authority and the interested parties against whom it is enforceable. Similarly, a planning obligation may be modified with the consent of the planning authority, where it would serve a useful planning purpose equally well with some modification proposed by the applicant. In the case of a planning authority's failure to determine an application to modify or discharge an obligation, or its decision to refuse such an application, there is a right of appeal to the Secretary of State.

Planning obligations may be enforced through the Courts by means of an injunction.

Planning obligations are the main means by which *planning gain* is achieved. However, as with the term 'Green Belt', which has statutory meaning, the expression 'planning gain' may mean different things to different people. It is widely misunderstood and is often mistakenly used to refer also to benefits which arise as a direct consequence of a development (for example, the removal of an eyesore) or, controversially, for some other form of benefit unrelated to the development (which the Government has made clear is not acceptable).

Further advice on this complex subject is set out in DoE Circular 1/97: Planning Obligations (England) and, in Wales, in the similarly titled WO Circular 13/97.

6.1 Planning appeals

An appeal should be an act of last resort and be considered only when all else has failed. Nevertheless, from time to time circumstances might arise where it is necessary to appeal against the planning authority's decision or its failure to determine an application.

Appeals are made to the Planning Inspectorate, an executive agency which is the main source of independent expertise for resolving disputes about the use of land, natural resources and the environment. Its role is governed by the three fundamental principles of openness, fairness and impartiality (the 'Franks' principles). Most of its Inspectors are graduates and members of professional bodies. They come from a variety of backgrounds which include planning, architecture, the environment, law and engineering. Inspectors are carefully selected, undergo rigorous training and work from home, with the support of office-based staff at the Inspectorate's headquarters in Bristol (or in Cardiff where appeals are dealt with on behalf of the National Assembly for Wales). Except in a relatively few cases where the Secretary of State has intervened, Inspectors are responsible for deciding appeals.

Appeals may be lodged against:

- the refusal of permission;
- conditions imposed on a permission or reserved matters approval which are considered unacceptable;
- the refusal to approve details submitted as a reserved matter, following the grant of an outline permission;
- the refusal to approve details arising from a condition of any planning permission;
- any requirement to submit further details in support of an outline application;
- the planning authority's failure to decide an application within the prescribed period (normally eight weeks, unless this is extended by agreement).

In addition, there are rights of appeal in respect of:

- removal or variation of conditions attached to a permission;
- listed building consent;
- conservation area consent;
- advertisement regulations consent;
- tree preservation order consent;
- hedgerow regulations consent;
- certificates of lawfulness (aka lawful development certificates – LDCs);
- enforcement notices.

Whether it is an appeal against a planning refusal, or some other special consent or decision, the broad issues that you should consider and the general principles and procedures involved are similar. However, it should be noted that the time limits for lodging an appeal can vary.

Unlike some other planning jurisdictions, for example in Ireland and the Isle of Man, there is no third party right of appeal against a planning authority's decision to grant permission (although this may be challenged by judicial review, as explained later).

6.1.1 Deciding whether to appeal

Even in the apparently most straightforward of cases, for example where there has been consistent officer support for the proposed development and it has been recommended for approval, but this has subsequently been overturned by Members, it is probably best to seek an independent opinion on the chances of success and other advice from an appropriate specialist, such as a planning consultant. But before doing that, it is crucial to study carefully the reasons for refusal given on the decision notice to see whether these relate to matters of principle or to technical objections that might be overcome by a revised proposal.

You should discuss the reasons for refusal with the planning officer who dealt with the application, to gauge the strength of the case that is likely to be mounted against the proposed development and seek an informal opinion on whether an amended scheme is likely to be acceptable. Most planning officers are used to looking at the arguments from both sides and will talk openly about relevant considerations, often acknowledging where a decision has been marginal and the issues finely balanced. Where the planning authority has had relevant experience of a similar appeal elsewhere within its area, this is likely to be brought to your attention.

Try to establish whether the planning authority would be prepared to accept an appeal by the exchange of written representations or would be more likely to seek a hearing or public inquiry, as these have a significant bearing on the cost and likely duration of the process (see below). In the event of a public inquiry, find out if this is likely to be handled by the council's own officers or, as is increasingly the case, whether consultants would be appointed. Also, ask whether the planning authority is likely to instruct Counsel or rely on its own in-house solicitor to act as advocate.

The strength of third party opposition should also be considered and, in particular, how they would be likely to respond to an appeal. Well organised and motivated objectors can be formidable opponents!

Also bear in mind the following:

- About one-third of all appeals are successful.
- There are strict time limits for lodging an appeal and for the subsequent process.
- An appeal can only be made by whoever has been named originally as the applicant (although this may of course be via an agent).
- An appeal for non-determination may result in a longer delay in securing permission that might otherwise have been the case, had the planning authority been allowed more time to consider the application.
- While lodging an appeal and submitting a revised proposal is not a mutually exclusive course of action, where this happens planning authorities may regard the former as an aggressive tactic and be less inclined to negotiate on the fresh application. On the other hand, some will argue that this enables the applicant to negotiate from a position of strength, on the basis that the planning authority might be tempted into settling for the 'lesser of two evils', and wish to avoid both the expense of the appeal, and risking its outcome. In such situations, the planning authority would normally expect an assurance to be given that the appeal would be withdrawn.

- Appeals can be lengthy, time-consuming and expensive (although there is no fee for making the appeal itself), especially where hearings and public inquiries are concerned. In the latter case, and also with enforcement appeals, it is possible to seek an award of costs against any party on the grounds of their unreasonable behaviour, although this is normally difficult to prove. Otherwise, the general rule is that parties are expected to pay their own expenses for an appeal, and these will depend on its complexity.
- An appeal can be withdrawn at any stage, but late withdrawal may result in costs against the appellant.
- An appeal against conditions can lead to others which have not been appealed being altered, further conditions added, or the loss of the entire permission itself (although the opportunity to withdraw the appeal will be given).

6.1.2 Choosing the right procedure

There are three types of procedure for dealing with planning appeals:

- written representations;
- hearing (commonly referred to, incorrectly, as an informal hearing);
- public inquiry.

Which procedure is followed will depend to a large extent on the particular circumstances of the case. Having said that, the Planning Inspectorate is at pains to point out that the choice of procedure has no bearing on the outcome of the appeal, which will always depend on its planning merits. However, it is worth considering the following:

- The written procedure is generally preferred by the Inspectorate and is the most popular. It is also usually quicker and cheaper. By definition, any weaknesses in the case can only be challenged in writing.
- A public inquiry may be requested by either the appellant or the planning authority or, because of the complexity of the issues and extent of any third party interest or local opposition, the Inspectorate may insist on this in any event.
- A public inquiry provides an opportunity to present the evidence in person before an Inspector and to test the evidence presented by the planning authority and others, through cross-examination. It is the most formal of the procedures and is similar to a court of law, although slightly less adversarial. Nevertheless, legal representation may often be appropriate or necessary.
- A hearing is more informal and, although questions may be asked, legal representation and formal cross-examination is not normally permitted.
- In the case of either a hearing or a public inquiry, there is a possibility of costs being awarded for unreasonable behaviour.

At the time of writing, the Planning Inspectorate is facing a possible backlog of casework following a substantial increase recently in planning appeals. This has caused difficulties, especially in dealing with the rising number of requests for hearings, which are taking significantly longer to process. The Chief Planning Inspector has therefore urged planning authorities and agents to consider very carefully whether hearings are really necessary and opt instead for the written procedure.

6.1.3 Time limits

Whichever procedure is chosen, it is essential to ensure that a valid, completed appeal is lodged within the relevant time limit. For normal planning appeals, this is six months from:

- the date of decision;
- the end of the eight-week period (in the case of an appeal against non-determination);
- the date when further details were requested in support of an outline application.

In addition, once the appeal has been lodged there is a strict timetable that must be adhered to, otherwise representations or other supporting documentation will be not normally be considered.

6.1.4 Written representations

About 75 per cent of appeals are dealt with by this method and the Inspectorate currently aims to process 80 per cent of such appeals within 16 weeks.

Initially, it involves completing an appeal form and submitting the following supporting documentation:

- A copy of the application to the planning authority.
- A copy of the relevant site ownership certificate and ownership details submitted with the planning application.
- A list of, and copies of, all relevant documents, drawings and plans which were part of the original planning application, including any environmental statement.
- Copies of any plans, drawings and documents submitted in support of, but not actually forming part of the application.
- Copies of any additional plans or drawings not previously seen by the planning authority.
- A copy of any decision by the LPA that the application has to be dealt with under the Environmental Impact Assessment Regulations 1999 (a 'screening opinion').
- Copies of all relevant correspondence (including any letters or drawings sent to the LPA changing the application).
- A copy of the LPA's decision (if issued).
- If the appeal relates to a condition, a copy of the original permission.
- A plan showing the site outlined in red, including two well-established named roads.
- If the appeal concerns approval of details imposed on an outline permission (that is, reserved matters) a copy of the original application for outline planning permission, the plan and the outline permission itself.

The most important part of the appeal form is the section that requires the 'grounds of appeal' to be set out. These should be set out in full and it may be necessary to do this in a separate document. It is not sufficient to merely contradict the reasons for refusal; each ground of appeal should be supported by a reasoned argument. If the Inspectorate considers that these are inadequate it will seek further details and this could delay the processing of the appeal. According to your experience of such matters and the issues involved, it might be wise to seek specialist advice from a planning consultant, although this may not be necessary in simple cases. In any event, it is important to ensure that submissions are clear, concise and business-like. Avoid extravagant or emotional language, and make sure that sufficient evidence is put forward to substantiate your claims.

Once the appeal has been validated, an acknowledgement letter is sent out giving the name of the case officer and an official starting date for the appeal (the date of the letter). The letter also sets out the timetable, which is essentially as follows:

- Within two weeks from the starting date, the planning authority must submit a copy of an appeal questionnaire and supporting documents, including relevant development plan policies, the planning officer's report to committee (if there is one) and copies of correspondence received from third parties. A copy of these papers is sent to the appellant. The questionnaire will identify whether the planning authority agrees to the written procedure and whether it intends to submit a further written statement. If it does (and this happens in the majority of cases) there will be an opportunity to comment on it.
- Within six weeks of the starting date, the appellant must submit two copies of any statement detailing the case in support of the grounds of appeal. However, this cannot be used as an opportunity to introduce new grounds of appeal. If the planning authority has indicated that it will be producing a similar statement of case, then two copies of this must also be submitted within this period. The Inspectorate will send each party a copy of the other's statement, together with copies of any correspondence received from interested persons in response to the requisite appeal notification procedures.
- Within nine weeks, both the planning authority and the appellant must submit to the Inspectorate two copies of any comments on each other's statement, or submissions by interested parties. However, no new evidence may be submitted at this stage. Any final comments are copied to the planning authority and appellant.

These deadlines are strictly enforced by the Inspectorate and any late submissions will normally be returned. At the end of this period, the appeal file is sent to the Inspector who will consider the appeal. Usually, within about 12 weeks of the starting date, arrangements are made for the Inspector to visit the site. If the site can be seen clearly from a public road and the parties have agreed, the Inspector will do this unaccompanied. However, where it is necessary for the Inspector to view the site from private land, he/she must be accompanied by the appellant (or his/her representative) and someone from the planning authority. If one party fails to arrive, the Inspector will carry out the inspection alone or another visit will be arranged. Any interested person who has commented on the appeal and wishes to attend will normally be allowed to do so.

At the site visit, the Inspector will introduce him/herself, check who is present, outline briefly the procedure and make sure that the parties agree that the Inspector is dealing with the correct set of plans. It will be stressed that the purpose of the visit is not to discuss the merits of the appeal or to listen to the arguments from any of the parties. Where someone fails to adhere to this advice, the Inspector will be quick to intervene or simply walk away from the person concerned. The Inspector will ask the parties whether there are any physical features on the site or in the vicinity to which they wish to draw attention, or to confirm any features referred to in the submissions. Occasionally, an Inspector may also look at the site from adjoining land (e.g. from an objector's property) but will need to be accompanied by the main parties.

In general, appeal decisions are issued within about five weeks of the Inspector's site visit. Most follow the same format and will:

- summarise the appeal details and decision;
- discuss briefly any procedural matters;
- summarise relevant development plan policy;
- identify the main issues and set out the reasons for the decision;
- include a note setting out the circumstances in which the validity of the decision may be challenged by application to the High Court.

At Appendix F is a diagram summarising the main stages in an appeal by the written procedure.

6.1.5 Hearings

In recent years, hearings have become increasingly popular and about 20 per cent of appeals are dealt with by this method. Although a hearing may be requested, it is up to the Inspectorate to decide whether this method would be appropriate bearing in mind how complicated or controversial the case is.

Currently, the average time for processing such appeals is about 22 weeks.

Hearings are quicker, cheaper and less formal than a public inquiry and usually involve a round table discussion led by the Inspector, based on previously submitted written statements (known as 'hearing statements'). The discussion may continue on the accompanied site visit. Legal representation is not normally allowed, and there is no formal cross-examination.

The hearing statement must set out the case that will be put forward at the hearing and include any maps or plans that will be referred to. In addition, it should include a list of any conditions or limitations, to which the appellant would agree, were the appeal to be allowed. The format for a statement for hearing cases may be found at Annex 2(i) of DETR Circular 05/2000: Planning Appeals – Procedures (Including Inquiries into Called-In Planning Applications) (England only).

Before the close of the hearing, the Inspector will ask whether any party wishes to make an application for costs. These may be awarded in the case of unreasonable behaviour, late withdrawal or the submission of late evidence.

If the appellant wishes to rely on a planning obligation, a final draft must be submitted at least five working days before the date of the hearing, and completed by the time it closes.

The timetable is essentially the same as for the written procedure. A hearing will normally be arranged within 12 weeks of the starting date.

6.1.6 Public Inquiries

Only about five per cent of appeals are dealt with by way of a public inquiry and, as an architect, it is unlikely that you will find yourself taking the lead in such an appeal. In most cases, a solicitor and/or planning consultant, probably acting together with Counsel, will assume overall responsibility for managing the appeal. Nevertheless, from time to time, architects are required to take the stand at a public inquiry to explain or defend their proposals, and it is therefore helpful to understand a little about the process.

The Inspectorate currently aims to decide 80 per cent of appeals by public inquiry within 30 weeks.

There are two different procedures according to whether the appeal is to be decided by the Inspector or the Secretary of State. In the case of the former, the public inquiry is normally held about 20 weeks after the starting date and, where the Secretary of State has intervened, after about 22 weeks.

In many respects, the early stages of the process are similar to those for other appeals, although where an expert witness proposes to read out a statement at the inquiry (in other words a 'proof of evidence') this must be submitted at least four weeks before the inquiry. If longer than 1,500 words, it should include a summary; usually only this will be read out at the inquiry. Also at least four weeks before the inquiry, a 'statement of common ground' must be submitted to the Inspectorate, detailing those points that have been discussed and agreed between the planning authority and the appellant.

At the inquiry, the planning authority will present its case first, with the advocate calling witnesses in turn. Each will present their evidence, either by reading out the 'summary proof', or by being led through their 'main proof' by the authority's advocate, examining the evidence briefly and perhaps reading out relevant extracts or answering specific questions. When this is complete, it is the turn of the appellant's advocate to cross-examine the planning authority's witness (that is, ask questions) in an attempt to test the evidence and expose its weaknesses. When this has finished, there is an opportunity for the planning authority's advocate to re-examine the witness in order to clarify any matters that arose during cross-examination. This is essentially an exercise in damage limitation, with the planning authority's advocate attempting to win back or play down any significant concessions made by the witness. Next, the Inspector may ask any questions of the witness.

When the planning authority has finished presenting its case, it is the turn of the appellant, following the same procedure. If there are interested persons present, for example objectors or representatives of amenity societies, etc they will normally be invited to have their say. The Inspector may also allow them to question witnesses and be questioned themselves.

At some stage in the inquiry there will normally be a discussion on suggested conditions and the terms of any planning obligation which might be under consideration.

Normally, both the appellant and the planning authority will make a closing statement, summing up their respective arguments and highlighting any points won or lost during the course of the inquiry. The appellant has the final say.

As in the case of hearings, any application for costs should be made before the close of the inquiry. Once the inquiry has closed, the Inspector will carry out an accompanied site inspection but, unlike the hearing procedure, is not able to listen to any further arguments about the merits of the proposed development. At this stage, the Inspector will simply be looking at the physical features on or near the site, to which attention may be drawn by the parties if necessary.

6.1.7 Costs

The parties to an appeal are normally expected to meet their own expenses. However, in the case of a hearing or public inquiry, either the appellant or the local planning authority can apply for costs if they feel that the other party has behaved 'unreasonably'. In addition, interested persons (that is, third parties) can seek an award of costs where a hearing or public inquiry has been cancelled at a late stage because of some unreasonable behaviour on the part of the appellant or planning authority, thus involving unnecessary expenditure in preparing for the appeal. Only in exceptional circumstances are third parties otherwise likely to be involved in making or facing a claim for costs.

Except for enforcement notice and lawful development certificate appeals, an application for costs cannot be made where an appeal is dealt with by exchange of written representations.

Costs awards are not dependent on the outcome of the appeal. Simply because an appeal succeeds it does not mean that the appellant is entitled to recover his expenses or conversely, if it fails, that he would be liable for paying the local planning authority costs. Nor will an application for costs influence the decision on the appeal, although there are some practitioners who consider that, in some circumstances, the overall planning case is strengthened by such a claim.

Applications for costs are dealt with separately from appeal decisions and usually follow at the end of the process. For an application to succeed, it must be made at the appropriate time, and one party must have behaved unreasonably and put the other party to an unnecessary expense. Examples of unreasonable behaviour include the following (the list is not exhaustive):

On the part of the local planning authority

- Failure to substantiate reasons for refusal (or those that would have been given had the application been determined) or for failing to make a decision.
- Refusing an application which accords with development plan policies, unless substantial evidence is provided to show other material considerations supporting such a refusal.
- Refusing an application on the grounds of prematurity without demonstrating how the emerging plan would be prejudiced.
- Imposing unreasonable conditions, or failing to consider the possibility of conditions or planning obligations as an alternative to refusing permission.
- Inhibiting or delaying a development which could reasonably have been permitted.
- Failing to comply with relevant appeal procedures, resulting in the hearing/inquiry being adjourned, unnecessarily prolonged or cancelled.

- Failure to take proper account of national planning advice and guidance or relevant judicial authority.
- Failure to take proper account of any relevant recent appeal decision or planning permission, where there has been no material change in circumstances.
- Refusing permission or reserved matters approval because of issues more appropriate to, or settled at, the outline stage – without good reason.
- Making unreasonable demands for infrastructure provision or planning obligations.
- Failure to renew a recently expired or extant planning permission, where there has been no material change in circumstances.
- Misapplying policies, applying out-of-date policies or attaching too much weight to emerging policies.
- Seeking to control the detailed design of buildings, unless this is justified by the locational characteristics of the proposed development.
- Refusing permission against professional or technical advice given by officers or statutory bodies or consultees, unless there are reasonable planning grounds for doing so.
- At a late stage introducing an additional reason for refusal, or withdrawing a reason for refusal.
- Refusing an application on the grounds of local opposition, unless it is founded upon valid planning reasons which are supported by substantial evidence.
- Refusing an application on the grounds of insufficient details, where these have not been sought.
- Failing to exercise discretion in enforcement proceedings: issuing an enforcement notice where it was not expedient to do so and there is no significant planning objection to the alleged breach of control.
- In certain circumstances, the withdrawal, or late withdrawal of an enforcement notice, or its incorrect drafting.
- Failure to discuss the application or the development alleged in an enforcement notice, or to provide reasonably requested information, where this would have avoided the need for an appeal.
- Failure to undertake adequate investigations of fact prior to serving an enforcement notice.

On the part of the appellant

- Failure to comply with procedural requirements, causing a hearing or inquiry to be adjourned, unnecessarily prolonged or cancelled.
- Late withdrawal of the appeal or grounds of appeal.
- Deliberately uncooperative behaviour.
- Failing to provide the required information in support of the appeal.
- Introducing new grounds of appeal or issues late in the proceedings.
- Persisting with an appeal where it is clear this would prejudice the outcome of the development plan process.
- Pursuing an appeal for development which is identical or very similar to that which has recently been dismissed on appeal in respect of the same site, or which flies in the face of national planning policies and has no reasonable chance of success.
- Failure to attend the hearing or inquiry.

Only a relatively small percentage of claims for costs succeed, such is the general reluctance of Inspectors to penalise parties, except in the most clear-cut of cases. Sometimes, a partial award of costs may be made.

The decision on an application for costs is made at the same time as the appeal decision. Neither the Secretary of State nor Inspectors determine the amount of any costs payable, which do not include any compensation for indirect losses suffered, for example as a result of the delay in obtaining permission. Where agreement cannot be reached between the parties on the amount of the award, the matter must be referred to a Taxing Officer of the Supreme Court for resolution.

Further information can be found in DoE Circular 8/93: Costs in Planning and other Proceedings (in Wales, WO Circular 23/93).

6.2 Challenges: statutory and judicial review

In effect, an appeal decision is final unless successfully challenged through the Courts – this procedure is known as 'statutory review'. However, such a challenge cannot be mounted simply because someone is unhappy with the outcome. It is necessary to demonstrate, for example, that an Inspector has failed to give adequate reasons for the decision or to consider a matter that ought to have been taken into account. Basic errors, such as failing to comply with relevant requirements or exceeding statutory powers, misinterpreting relevant legislation or policy guidance, or misunderstanding the application in some fundamental way, are also grounds for a challenge. If the challenge is successful, the decision will be quashed and the case remitted to the Secretary of State for re-determination. But that does not necessarily mean that the original decision will be reversed (although in some cases it will), simply that in the new decision the defect will be corrected.

Statutory challenges may only be made by 'a person aggrieved' by the decision and this can include not only the appellant but, in the case of an appeal which has been allowed, third parties and the local planning authority.

Applications to the High Court for leave to challenge an appeal decision must be made within six weeks from the date of decision. Because of the complexity and financial consequences of embarking on such a course of action, legal advice should always be sought beforehand.

Although there are significant differences, there is a similar right to challenge the decision of a local planning authority 'on a point of law'. This is known as 'judicial review'. Because this procedure is rarely appropriate where the right of appeal exists against a planning refusal, a judicial review is normally only brought by a third party against a planning approval. As with the statutory review, leave to pursue the challenge must be granted by the court and the applicant must establish sufficient *locus standii* (that is the right to take action or be heard by a court). An application for a judicial review must be made promptly and in any event within three months; anyone considering such action should therefore take legal advice as soon as it is known that an application is likely to be, or has been, approved.

6.3 Complaints to the council or Ombudsman

Both the Planning Inspectorate and local planning authorities have procedures for dealing with complaints about the way in which an appeal or application has been handled.

In serious cases, where an applicant or appellant feels that they have been treated unfairly through maladministration or have had problems in obtaining access to official information, it might be necessary to consider making a complaint to:

- *In the case of the Planning Inspectorate*, the Parliamentary Ombudsman (also called the Parliamentary Commissioner for Administration). The Ombudsman cannot be approached direct and will only deal with a matter once it has been referred by an MP. Although the Ombudsman can make various recommendations, he is not able to alter the Inspector's decision in any way.
- *In the case of a local planning authority*, the Local Government Ombudsman (there are separate ombudsmen for England and Wales). Complaints must be about maladministration, but only where this has caused significant injustice to the complainant (this includes financial loss or other hardship). The Ombudsman will not consider a complaint if the injustice is not great enough to justify an investigation, or where the matter is the subject of a planning appeal or review by the Courts.

Maladministration covers such things as unreasonable delay, failure to adhere to the authority's own rules or the law, bias, the use of improper considerations, the giving of wrong information and many other matters; but the actual merits of any decision will not be investigated. The procedures in England and Wales differ only slightly.

In England, before the Ombudsman can investigate a complaint, the council must first be given a reasonable opportunity to deal with the matter. This is normally done through a councillor. Complaints must be made within 12 months of the matter becoming known and made in writing, with supporting documentation. The Ombudsman will notify the council of the complaint, and invite its comments, and where appropriate carry out an investigation and produce a report and recommendation. Councils are not obliged to accept the Ombudsman's recommendations, but in nearly every instance they will.

In successful cases, recommended remedies can include the council having to make payments to the complainant, for example, where some loss in property value has resulted, together with meeting the costs of pursuing the complaint. It should be noted, however, that as the Ombudsman does not consider that it is usually necessary to use a professional advisor's services in order to make a complaint, it is unlikely to ask the council to pay such fees, other than in exceptional circumstances.

For further information, visit www.lgo.org.uk (The Commissioner for Local Administration in England), or www.ombudsman-wales.org (The Commissioner for Local Administration in Wales).

6.4 Human rights

Since the principles of the European Convention on Human Rights were enshrined within the Human Rights Act 1998, which came into force in October 2000, it is sometimes argued that the planning system has violated an individual's human rights in one way or another. Generally, these arise from claims that there has been a breach in:

- Article 1 of the First Protocol, which deals with the peaceful enjoyment of one's possessions and protection of property.
- Article 6, which is the procedural right to a fair trial.
- Article 8 which confers a qualified right to respect for private and family life and for the home.

In May 2001 the House of Lords upheld the procedures whereby the Secretary of State determines appeals and other cases, ruling that these were consistent with Article 6 of the Act.

Claims in the European Court that there has been a violation of a person's human rights have rarely succeeded and only in circumstances where the interference in the right of the individual concerned is not outweighed by the public interest, such as the preservation of the environment.

7.1 Before you start

A permission will lapse unless development is started within the specified time limit. The Courts have ruled that the commencement of development includes various operations, such as certain site clearance and ground works.

But before development is commenced, it is essential to check that all relevant planning conditions have been complied with. Failure to comply with any condition which requires something to be done before building work starts can result in a failure to keep the permission alive. This means that the development is unauthorised, and exposes the risk of enforcement action.

7.2 Changes

It is quite common, once permission has been granted, for developments to change: in response to the altered requirements of the client, the need to satisfy other statutory codes such as building or fire regulations, or simply because of some consideration or oversight on the part of the builder, during construction. In other cases, development might proceed with no permission at all, either unwittingly because it is incorrectly assumed that permission is not required, or sometimes in a deliberate attempt to flout the system. However, while it is not a criminal offence to carry out development without first obtaining the necessary authorisations (other than in certain cases, including where listed building, conservation area or TPO consent is required), generally this is not a good idea and may cause significant problems when valuing or trying to dispose of the land concerned.

Minor changes to a permission can often be dealt with quite simply by sending a letter and a copy of the revised drawings to the planning officer who handled the application, who will normally consider the matter under delegated powers. However, where the changes are material, it will be necessary to submit a revised planning application. In addition, as explained earlier at 5.4.4, Section 73A of the 1990 Act specifically enables an application to be made retrospectively to regularise an unauthorised development, although this cannot be done in the case of listed building or conservation area consent.

7.3 Breaches of planning control

Local planning authorities are equipped with various powers to remedy serious breaches in planning control and these include:

- The power to serve a 'planning contravention notice' where it appears that there has been a breach of planning control and the LPA requires further information about activities on the land and details of ownership/occupation. In effect, this is often a shot across the bows.
- The power to serve an 'enforcement notice' to require certain steps to be taken to remedy any breach of planning control, or for specified activities to cease, within a stated period for compliance.
- The power to serve a 'breach of condition notice' where there is failure to comply with any condition or limitation imposed on a grant of planning permission. The period for compliance

is normally 28 days, unless a longer period is agreed, and failure to do so is a finable offence.
- The ability to seek a court 'injunction' to restrain any actual or expected breach of planning control.
- The power to serve a 'stop notice' to prohibit the use of land, for example as the site for a caravan occupied as a person's only or main residence, and to make a stop notice immediately effective where special reasons justify it.

Powers are also available to enforce against breaches of the special controls relating to listed building, conservation area, tree preservation order, hedgerow and advertisement regulations and other consents.

Local planning authorities have a general discretion to take enforcement action, when they consider it 'expedient' to remedy a breach of control that would cause serious harm to public amenity or some other interest of acknowledged importance. They should not therefore instigate formal enforcement proceedings against a minor breach of control which causes no harm to local amenity. In addition, any enforcement action should always be proportionate to the breach of planning control and follow efforts to persuade the owner or occupier of the site to voluntarily remedy the harmful effects of unauthorised development, including where it might be made acceptable by the imposition of conditions, inviting the submission of a planning application. Local authorities are encouraged to exercise particular care when considering enforcement proceedings against small businesses, the self-employed and private householders.

There are potentially significant penalties for contravening the requirements of an effective enforcement notice, or the prohibition in a stop notice. Following successful prosecution in the Courts, a convicted person can be fined up to £20,000 and the extent of such a fine will take into account any financial benefit which has accrued, or appears likely to accrue, as a consequence of the offence.

While there is a right of an appeal in the usual way against an enforcement notice, no similar appeal can be made to the Secretary of State (or National Assembly of Wales) against a breach of condition notice, stop notice or injunction. Where an appeal against an enforcement notice is contemplated, bear in mind:

- anyone with a legal interest in the land the subject of the notice is entitled to appeal (that is, owner, tenant, etc);
- the completed appeal must be lodged before the notice takes effect (this is usually 28 days after it has been served);
- once the appeal has been lodged, the notice is suspended pending its outcome;
- it is possible to appeal on various legal and planning grounds, and thus it is advisable to seek the advice of a planning consultant or planning solicitor;
- the appeal includes a deemed application for planning permission;
- a fee is normally payable to both the Inspectorate and the local planning authority;
- in certain circumstances, costs may be awarded where one party to the appeal has behaved unreasonably.

There are time limits for taking enforcement action against breaches in planning control, after which the development becomes 'immune' from such proceedings. In short, these are:

- operational development (see 5.1 for definition) – four years from the date that these were substantially completed;
- change of use to a single dwellinghouse – four years from the date of the breach in control;
- all other breaches of planning control, including material changes in the use of land and any breach of condition or limitation of a planning permission – ten years.

However, there are *no* time limits for issuing listed building or conservation area enforcement notices.

Further general information on enforcement may be found in PPG18: Enforcing Planning Control, issued in December 1991, and more detailed advice in the similarly titled DOE Circular 10/97.

The Government appears hell-bent on reforming the planning system in order to reduce bureaucracy, simplify plan-making, speed things up and engage the public more effectively. For the purposes of this *Guide*, in England the most relevant changes signalled by the planning reform paper: *Sustainable Communities – Delivering through Planning*, and the emerging Planning and Compulsory Purchase Bill, are as follows.

8.1 Generally

- The goal of 'sustainable development' will be made a statutory purpose of planning.
- Existing policy guidance will be reviewed over the course of the next three years to reduce the volume and increase its clarity.
- An enabling power in primary legislation will be sought for the Secretary of State to prescribe a timetable for called-in and recovered appeal decisions.
- The Government will issue clear statements of national policy on major infrastructure projects and implement ways to make public inquiries more efficient. It has, however, abandoned its earlier plans to introduce a Parliamentary Procedure.
- Regional Planning Guidance will be replaced by a statutory Regional Spatial Strategy.
- County councils will lose their strategic planning powers and structure plans are to be abolished.
- Local Development Frameworks (LDFs) will replace local development plans and unitary development plans. LDFs will include a proposals map. Joint LDFs can be prepared between districts or with counties.
- A new 'Best Value indicator' to cover plan-making will be introduced and the Government is proposing to use its intervention powers where necessary.
- So-called Business Planning Zones (BPZs) are proposed.
- Compulsory purchase will be made simpler, fairer and quicker, by strengthening powers, improving compensation arrangements and speeding up the procedures

8.2 Development control

- A statement of development principles, which might eventually replace outline planning permission, will be introduced.
- The validity of a planning permission will be reduced to three years.
- The General Permitted Development Order is to be updated.
- Local development orders are to be introduced.
- Local authorities will be given powers to refuse repeat applications.
- 'Twin-tracking' will be banned, but only after substantive improvements have been made to deal with planning applications.
- Policy guidance on s. 106 agreements (see 5.10) will be revised.
- The processing of planning applications will be made more efficient.
- A target for the percentage of decisions made under delegated powers will be set and a checklist of matters that need to be included in applications introduced. The Government is also taking forward work on 'delivery contracts'.
- The efficiency of appeal process will be improved, including reducing the time for an applicant to decide whether to lodge an appeal to three months.

- A statutory deadline of 21 days to respond to pre-application requests for advice will be introduced.
- The number and the types of development for which statutory consultees should be consulted will be reviewed, although there is no presumption that the list would be reduced.
- The use of standing advice by statutory consultees will be encouraged.
- Appropriate targets and monitoring for consultees sponsored by Government departments will be considered.
- Financial assistance to Planning Aid will be provided.
- The Government will make the handling of planning applications more transparent. It will require local authorities to give reasons for their decisions to approve planning applications and make sure that local people have cheap and easy access to applications and other documents about planning.
- Enforcement procedures will be reviewed and be the subject of a consultation document.

8.3 In Wales

Wales is pushing ahead with similar plans to reform the planning system. Although based on the same legislation, the planning system in Wales is different from that in England, and therefore the Welsh Assembly Government has carried out its own separate consultation. *Planning: Delivering for Wales*, published in February 2002, sets out the Assembly's proposals to improve the operation of the planning system in Wales. It proposes making it a statutory requirement for the Assembly to prepare the Wales Spatial Plan; to replace unitary development plans with more focused, quickly-prepared local development plans; and to improve the development control process to enable it to deliver clear, consistent decisions.

There has been widespread support for the proposals, particularly improvements to the development plan system, for local Member and officer training, for the preparation of the Wales Spatial Plan and for more resources to be made available for the planning service.

NB. For the further information on plans to reform the English and Welsh planning systems, including the latest on emerging legislation, check out the ODPM and National Assembly for Wales websites (see Appendix A).

Some final thoughts...

For any small practice, stepping into the planning maze can prove to be a daunting experience. Hopefully, this *Guide* will help. But we are sure that you will not fall into the biggest trap, having read it through cover to cover, that now you 'know it all'! There may still be a few blind alleys ahead and unseen pits to trip into. It therefore makes good sense to cultivate a working relationship with a local planning consultant to whom you can go for additional help, advice and guidance. After all, you would not attempt brain surgery all by yourself using only a surgeon's 'do-it-yourself-kit'. And by now, you will have realised that involvement in the planning process can be just as complex and perilous, and perhaps for some of your clients faced with a planning refusal the effect could appear just as fatal.

In his companion RIBA Publications Small Practices series, *A Guide to Working with Consultants*, Neil Parkyn explores the relationships between architects and consultants and shows you ways of working better together. As he says, 'Collaboration between architects, consultants or sub-consultants at its best can be magical.' And so it can be with specialist planning consultants, and as fruitful too we consider. We suggest that you read, digest and follow his good advice.

National planning guidance

The following may be obtained by visiting the website of the Office of Deputy Prime Minister (ODPM) at www.odpm.gov.uk (for English guidance) and the National Assembly for Wales at www.wales.gov.uk (for Welsh guidance).

For England

These are the current Planning Policy Guidance Notes (PPGs).

PPG1:   General Policy and Principles (February 1997)
PPG2:   Green Belts (January 1995)
PPG3:   Housing (March 2000)
PPG4:   Industrial and Commercial Development and Small Firms (November 1992)
PPG5:   Simplified Planning Zones (November 1992)
PPG6:   Town Centres and Retail Development (June 1996)
PPG7:   The Countryside – Environmental Quality and Economic and Social Development
          (February 1997)
PPG8:   Telecommunications (August 2001)
PPG9:   Nature Conservation (October 1994)
PPG10: Planning and Waste Management (February 1997)
PPG11: Regional Planning (October 2000)
PPG12: Development Plans (December 1999)
PPG13: Transport (March 1994)
PPG14: Development on Unstable Land (April 1990)
PPG15: Planning and the Historic Environment (September 1994)
PPG16: Archaeology and Planning (November 1990)
PPG17: Planning for Open Space, Sport and Recreation (July 2002)
PPG18: Enforcing Planning Control (December 1991)
PPG19: Outdoor Advertisement Control (March 1992)
PPG20: Coastal Planning (September 1992)
PPG21: Tourism (November 1992)
PPG22: Renewable Energy (February 1993)
PPG23: Planning and Pollution Control (July 1994)
PPG24: Planning and Noise (September 1994)
PPG25: Development and Flood Risk (July 2001)

For Wales

These documents are part of a series of Technical Advice Notes (Wales) (TANs) which supplement Planning Guidance (Wales): Planning Policy (March 2002).

TAN1   Joint Housing Land Availability Studies (October 1997)
TAN2   Planning and Affordable Housing (1996)
TAN3   Simplified Planning Zones (1996)
TAN4   Retailing and Town Centres (1996)

TAN5   Nature Conservation and Planning (1996)
TAN6   Agricultural and Rural Development (June 2000)
TAN7   Outdoor Advertisement Control (1996)
TAN8   Renewable Energy (1996)
TAN9   Enforcement of Planning Control (1997)
TAN10 Tree Preservation Orders (1997)
TAN11 Noise (1997)
TAN12 Design (2002)
TAN13 Tourism (1997)
TAN14 Coastal Planning (1998)
TAN15 Development and Flood Risk (1998)
TAN16 Sport and Recreation (1998)
TAN17 Environmental Assessment (1997)
TAN18 Transport (1998)
TAN19 Telecommunications (2002)
TAN20 The Welsh Language – Unitary Development Plans and Planning Control (June 2000)
TAN21 Waste (November 2001)

Regional Planning Guidance (England only)

RPG1   Strategic Guidance for the North East 1993
RPG3   Strategic Guidance for London 1996 (Supplemented by RPG3A London – Strategic Views and RPG3B/9B Strategic Planning Guidance for the River Thames)
RPG6   Strategic Guidance for East Anglia 2000
RPG8   Regional Planning Guidance for the East Midlands Region 2002
RPG9   Regional Planning Guidance for the South East Region 2001
RPG10 Regional Planning Guidance for the South West 2001
RPG11 Regional Planning Guidance for the West Midlands 1998
RPG12 Regional Planning Guidance for Yorkshire & Humberside 2001
RPG13 Regional Planning Guidance for the North West 1996

Major and other reference works

Two indispensable works for anyone proposing to become heavily involved in planning matters are:

- *Encyclopaedia of Planning Law and Practice* (an exhaustive seven-volume reference work published by Sweet & Maxwell; visit www.smlawpub.co.uk).
- *Development Control Practice* (published by Development Control Services Ltd).

The latter company also maintains a very large computer database of appeal decisions, known as COMPASS, which may be searched (for a fee) and selected copies acquired (go to www.dcservices.co.uk).

Planning is the weekly magazine for planning practitioners and is also the official journal of the RTPI. However, subscriptions are available to non-members. In addition to having a comprehensive news section, there is a weekly bulletin of the most important planning appeals decisions and a Development Control Casebook Forum where readers' queries are answered. There is a related website that includes many of the magazine's features at www.planning.haynet.com

The RTPI Library and Information Service (RTPI-LIS) includes a reference-only library collection of mainly post-1990 publications on planning-related topics, including a wide-ranging collection of current UK local plans, and 100 current periodicals. The online catalogue includes details of library holdings (excluding current legislation), a comprehensive index to journal articles, and details of Institute publications and policy statements since 1914. The library operates an enquiry service, including the compilation of subject reading lists, and can offer advice on alternative sources of information as required. Contact library@rtpi.org.uk or phone 020 7929 9452/9485.

A very comprehensive bibliography of reference sources and websites may be found at the University of Nottingham Online Planning Resources (www.nottingham.ac.uk/sbe/planbiblios).

The Council for the Protection of Rural England (CPRE) publishes a series of low cost, easy-to-understand guides and leaflets, and while aimed at campaigners, will be of interest to others engaged in the planning process. Their publication list may be viewed at www.cpre.org.uk

Planning Aid

Planning Aid is a free, voluntary service, offering independent professional advice and assistance on town planning matters. It is aimed at individuals, community groups and other voluntary groups who cannot afford to pay for commercial consultancy services. It can help people with their own planning applications or to comment on other people's applications. It is *not* a substitute for the services provided by local planning authorities, or for the services of a professional planning consultant. For information, contact the RTPI at www.rtpi.org.uk

The Planning Portal

The Planning Portal is the brainchild of the Planning Inspectorate and is being developed in partnership with a number of local authorities, the ODPM and the National Assembly for Wales. Although it only went live at the end of May 2002 and is in the early stages of development, it already presents a whole volume and range of information in a user-friendly form, 'avoiding technical language wherever possible'. A Welsh translation is ongoing.

The Planning Portal aims to explain in simple terms how the planning system works in England and Wales, contains a very useful glossary, and will eventually provide a conduit through which information on all the development plans – local, regional and national – in all the planning authorities can be accessed online. In addition, in the not too distant future a number of authorities will be able to receive applications online and their progress may be followed through the Planning Portal. The Inspectorate too are developing their Planning Casework Service, enabling the public to make and monitor planning appeals electronically.

Visit www.planningportal.gov.uk

Useful websites

There is a plethora of useful websites dealing with planning-related matters. Here are just a few:

Office of Deputy Prime Minister (ODPM) www.odpm.gov.uk
The Planning Directorate of the ODPM is responsible for the system of town and country planning, while the Government Offices for the Regions are closely involved in the preparation of regional guidance. This site includes details of current national planning policy, circulars, and related planning information and guidance.

National Assembly for Wales www.wales.gov.uk
This site functions in much the same way as the ODPM site for England and includes current Welsh planning policy and guidance.

Royal Town Planning Institute www.rtpi.org.uk
The RTPI is the professional institute for town planners. The site provides access to the Planning Consultants Referral Service, a free service providing a suitable list of firms to assist with town planning matters, the Library and Information Service (see above), and has good links to other sites.

Online Directory of Planning Consultants www.rtpiconsultants.co.uk

The Planning Inspectorate www.planning-inspectorate.gov.uk
In addition to publishing a number of very helpful guides to the different appeals that can be lodged, this site has a useful selection of links to other sites.

Planning Magazine www.planning.haynet.com

RIBANET www.ribanet.conference.com
This is an online conferencing facility for RIBA members. They can register free at this site. By August 2002, 3,500 members were connected. Included is a 'Planning' topic area. Members discuss individual planning issues and share their experiences of dealing with local planning authorities. For example: enforcement requiring the removal of PVC windows and their replacement with timber framed windows in a listed building.

'On-line planning aid service' www.planning-applications.co.uk
This is not an official RTPI sponsored Planning Aid site, but goes under the RICS banner.

Oultwood www.oultwood.com (an index to local government sites).

The Prince's Foundation www.princes-foundation.org
This site has an extensive list of links to architecture and planning-related websites.

British Urban Regeneration Association www.bura.org.uk

Civic Trust www.civictrust.org.uk

Commission for Architecture and the Built Environment www.cabe.org.uk

Countryside Agency www.countryside.gov.uk

Department for Culture, Media and Sport (DCMS) www.culture.gov.uk

English Heritage www.english-heritage.org.uk
An excellent range of services and publications is available here.

CADW (Welsh Historic Monuments) www.cadw.wales.gov.uk
The Welsh equivalent.

Department for Environment, Food and Rural affairs www.defra.gov.uk

Department for Trade & Industry www.dti.gov.uk

English Nature www.english-nature.org.uk

English Partnerships www.englishpartnerships.co.uk

Environment Agency www.environment-agency.gov.uk

Government Offices for the Regions www.government-offices.gov.uk

Health and Safety Executive www.hse.gov.uk

Her Majesty's Stationery Office (HMSO) www.hmso.gov.uk
A good place to look for legislation, statutory instruments, etc.

British and Irish Legal Information Institute www.bailii.org
Useful site for recent legislation and court cases.

Highways Agency www.highways.gov.uk

The Institution of Civil Engineers www.ice.org.uk

Landscape Institute www.l-i.org.uk

Law Society www.lawsoc.org.uk

Local Government Association www.lga.gov.uk

The Lord Chancellor's Department www.lcd.gov.uk

Ordnance Survey www.ordsvy.gov.uk
Main supplier of maps for planning applications, etc.

Planning Exchange www.planex.co.uk

The Planning Officers Society www.planningofficers.org.uk

Royal Institute of British Architects www.architecture.com

Royal Institution of Chartered Surveyors www.rics.org.uk

RUDI (Resource for Urban Design Information) www.rudi.net

Town and Country Planning Association www.tcpa.org.uk

The Commissioner for Local Administration in England (Ombudsman) www.lgo.org.uk

The Commissioner for Local Administration in Wales (Ombudsman) www.ombudsman-wales.org

The Parliamentary Commissioner for Administration (PCA) www.ombudsman.org.uk

Urban Design Alliance (UDAL) www.udal.org.uk

Appendix B

1. Development within the curtilage of a dwellinghouse
2. Minor operations
3. Changes of use
4. Temporary buildings and uses
5. Caravan sites
6. Agricultural buildings and operation
7. Forestry buildings and operations
8. Industrial and warehouse development
9. Repairs to unadopted streets and private ways
10. Repairs to services
11. Development under local or private Acts or Orders
12. Development by local authorities
13. Development by local highway authorities
14. Development by drainage bodies
15. Development by National Rivers Authority
16. Development by or on behalf of sewerage undertakers
17. Development by statutory undertakers
18. Aviation development
19. Development ancillary to mining operations
20. Coal mining development by the Coal Authority and licensed operators
21. Waste tipping at a mine
22. Mineral exploration
23. Removal of material from mineral-working deposits
24. Development by telecommunications code system operators
25. Other telecommunications development
26. Development by the Historic Buildings and Monuments Commission for England
27. Use by members of certain recreational organisations
28. Development at amusement parks
29. Driver information systems
30. Toll roads facilities
31. Demolition of buildings
32. Schools, colleges, universities and hospitals
33. Closed circuit television cameras

Note: For an on-line 'interactive' guide to Permitted Development,
visit www.planning-applications.co.uk

The Town and Country Planning (Use Classes) Order 1987, as amended: Summary of Use Classes (refer to Order for details and restrictions).

Appendix C

A1 Shops: including retail warehouses, hairdressers, undertakers, travel and ticket agencies, post offices, domestic hire shops, sandwich bars, etc but *excluding* amusement centres, laundrettes, motor fuel, motor vehicles and car hire, and the sale of hot food.

A2 Financial and professional services: including banks, building societies, estate and employment agencies, betting offices, professional and financial services, etc but *excluding* health and medical services.

A3 Food and drink: restaurants, pubs, wine bars, cafes, snack bars, hot food take-aways.

B1 Business: (a) offices not within A2
(b) research and development
(c) light industry

being a use which can be carried out in any residential area 'without detriment to the amenity of that area by reason of noise, vibration, smell, fumes, smoke, soot, ash, dust or grit'.

B2 General industrial: industrial processes not falling within class B1.

B8 Storage or distribution.

C1 Hotels.

C2 Residential institutions: including residential accommodation where a significant element of care is provided such as nursing homes and hospitals. Residential schools, colleges and training centres also fall within this class.

C3 Dwellinghouses: includes not more than six residents living together as a single household (including where care is provided) and communal housing for elderly or handicapped, unless a significant element of care is provided.

D1 Non-residential institutions: includes clinics, health centres, crèches, day nurseries/centres, non-residential schools, education and training centres, museums, public halls, libraries, art galleries, exhibition halls, places of worship and church halls.

D2 Assembly and leisure: includes cinemas, casinos, concert, bingo, dance and sports halls, swimming baths, skating rinks, gymnasia, other indoor or outdoor sports or recreations, excluding motorised vehicles or firearms.

Sui generis uses: These are uses which do not fall within any specified class and include:

- theatres;
- amusement centres;
- laundrettes;
- the sale of motor fuel;

- car showrooms;
- car hire;
- taxi businesses;
- scrapyards;
- hostels.

Note: The UCO provides that a move between activities within the same class is not development and therefore does not require planning permission. The Town and Country Planning (General Permitted Development) Order 1995 (as amended) (GPDO) also specifies certain moves between the Use Classes as 'permitted development', thus not requiring express planning permission.

At the time of writing, the Government is consulting on proposals to overhaul the Order with radical changes to the A classes of town centre uses.

Pre-deposit consultation

Public consultation on issues or draft proposals

Objections and representations

First deposit

Publication of deposit draft plan → Objections and representations → Planning authority considers objections → Pre-inquiry changes published

Second deposit*

Publication of revised deposit draft plan → Objections and representations → Planning authority considers objections → Pre-inquiry changes published

Public examination

Public inquiry/Examination-in-public (EIP)

Inspector's/Panel report

Report by Inspector/EIP panel

Modification

Planning authority considers report and recommended modifications → Proposed modifications on deposit → Objections and representations

Final stages

Possible further public inquiry/EIP ← Planning authority considers objections and further modifications

Report by Inspector/EIP panel → Statement of decisions on modifications

Adoption

Plan adopted

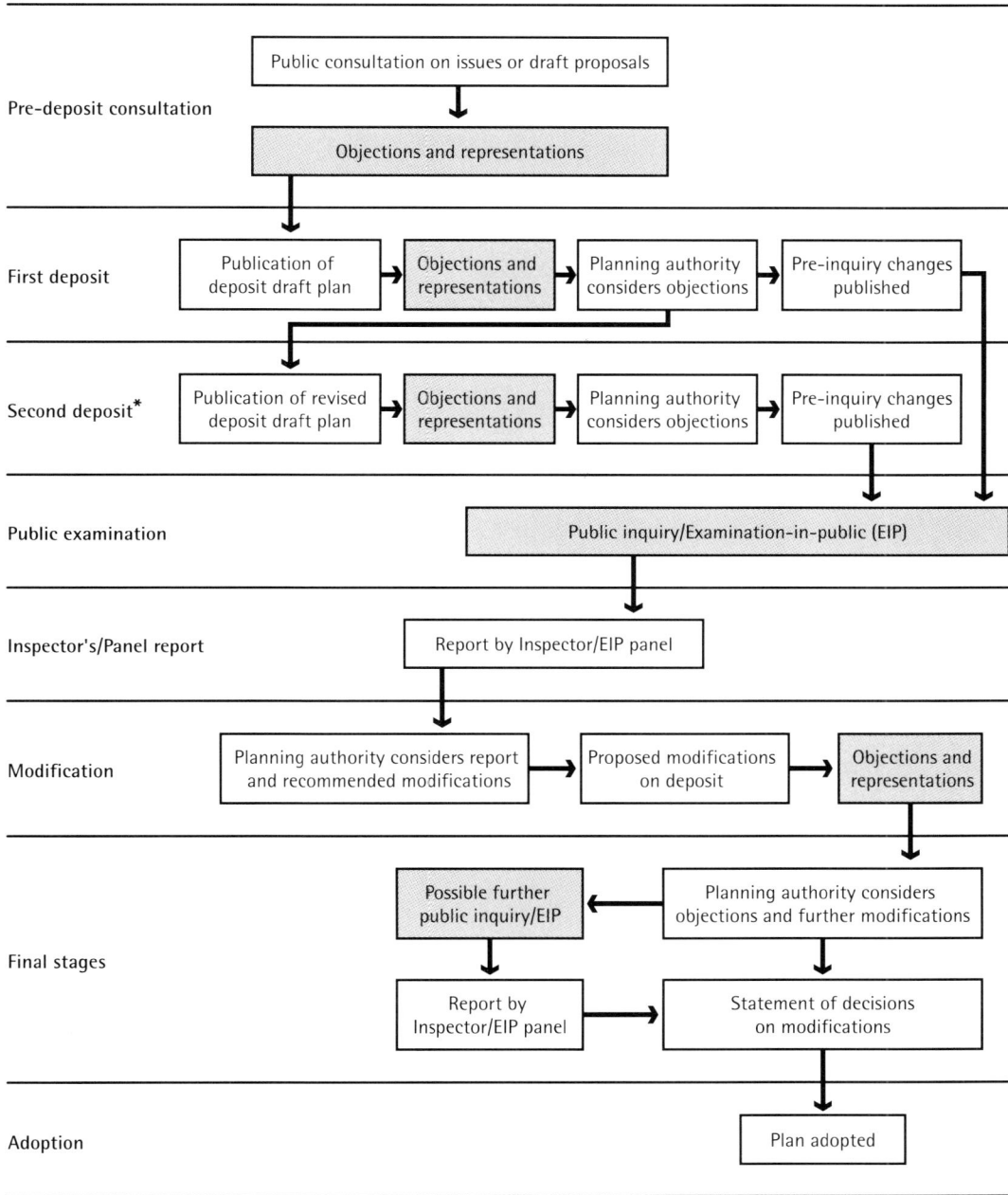

*Note: In the case of Structure Plans and Welsh UDPs, there is a single deposit stage only

A Guide to Negotiating the Planning Maze

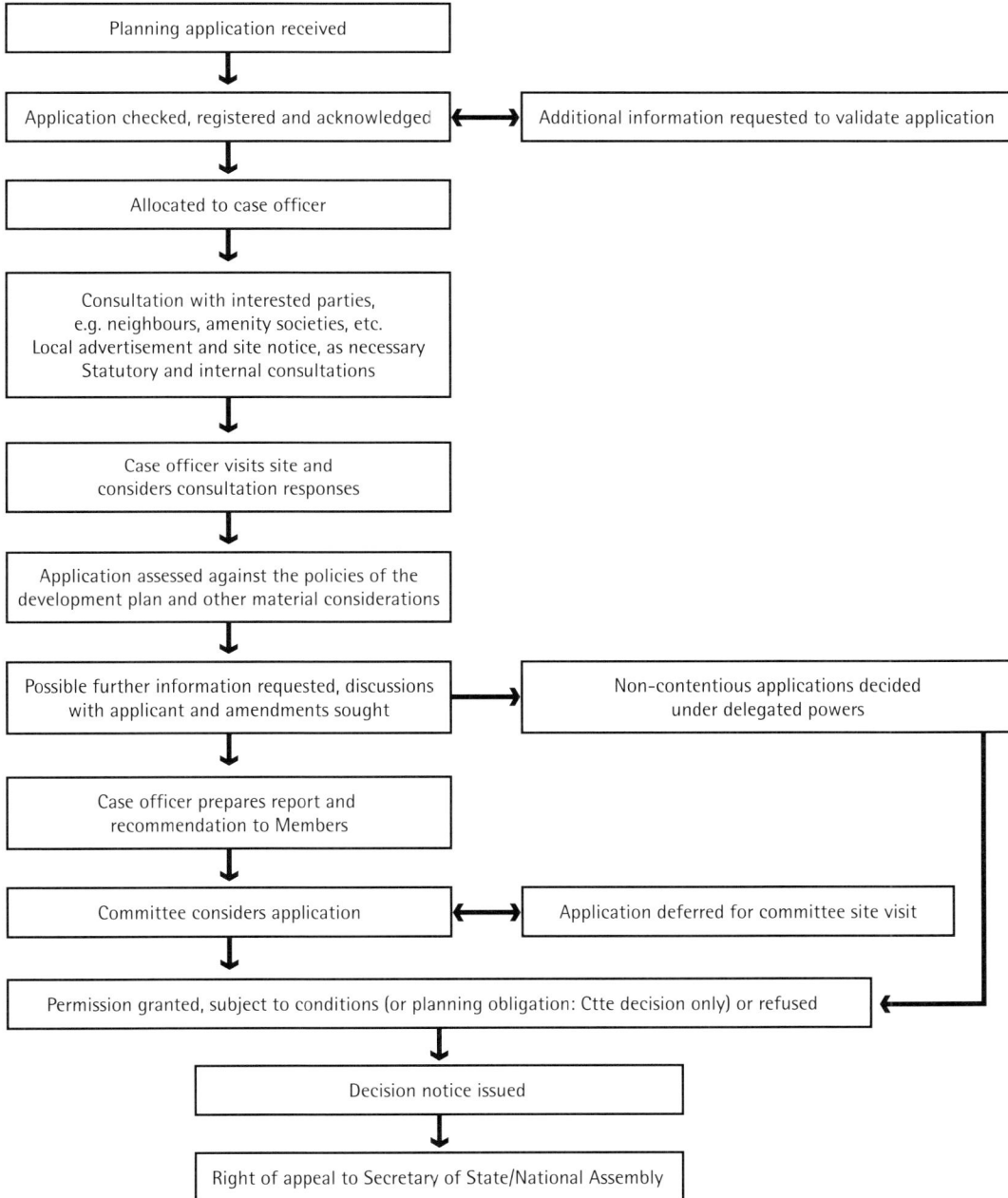

```
┌─────────────────────────────────────┐
│    Planning application received    │
└─────────────────────────────────────┘
                  │
                  ▼
┌─────────────────────────────────────┐        ┌──────────────────────────────────────────────┐
│ Application checked, registered and │◄──────►│ Additional information requested to validate   │
│           acknowledged              │        │                application                     │
└─────────────────────────────────────┘        └──────────────────────────────────────────────┘
                  │
                  ▼
┌─────────────────────────────────────┐
│        Allocated to case officer    │
└─────────────────────────────────────┘
                  │
                  ▼
┌─────────────────────────────────────┐
│    Consultation with interested     │
│        parties,                     │
│ e.g. neighbours, amenity societies, │
│            etc.                     │
│ Local advertisement and site notice,│
│         as necessary                │
│ Statutory and internal consultations│
└─────────────────────────────────────┘
                  │
                  ▼
┌─────────────────────────────────────┐
│      Case officer visits site and   │
│   considers consultation responses  │
└─────────────────────────────────────┘
                  │
                  ▼
┌─────────────────────────────────────┐
│ Application assessed against the    │
│ policies of the development plan and│
│ other material considerations       │
└─────────────────────────────────────┘
                  │
                  ▼
┌─────────────────────────────────────┐        ┌──────────────────────────────────────────────┐
│ Possible further information        │───────►│   Non-contentious applications decided         │
│ requested, discussions with         │        │          under delegated powers                │
│ applicant and amendments sought     │        └──────────────────────────────────────────────┘
└─────────────────────────────────────┘                              │
                  │                                                    │
                  ▼                                                    │
┌─────────────────────────────────────┐                              │
│    Case officer prepares report and │                              │
│    recommendation to Members        │                              │
└─────────────────────────────────────┘                              │
                  │                                                    │
                  ▼                                                    │
┌─────────────────────────────────────┐        ┌──────────────────────────────────────────────┐
│  Committee considers application    │◄──────►│ Application deferred for committee site visit  │
└─────────────────────────────────────┘        └──────────────────────────────────────────────┘
                  │                                                    │
                  ▼                                                    │
┌───────────────────────────────────────────────────────────────────┐│
│ Permission granted, subject to conditions (or planning obligation: │◄┘
│ Ctte decision only) or refused                                     │
└───────────────────────────────────────────────────────────────────┘
                  │
                  ▼
┌─────────────────────────────────────┐
│       Decision notice issued        │
└─────────────────────────────────────┘
                  │
                  ▼
┌─────────────────────────────────────┐
│ Right of appeal to Secretary of     │
│ State/National Assembly             │
└─────────────────────────────────────┘
```

Timetable	Appellant	Local Planning Authority (LPA)	Interested persons
Appeal lodged within the **6-month** time limit and official starting date set by Inspectorate.	Submits form, grounds of appeal and all supporting documents to Planning Inspectorate and LPA.	Accepts written procedure or requests hearing or inquiry.	
Within **2 weeks** from the starting date.	Receives the LPA's questionnaire and any supporting documents.	LPA sends out questionnaire and supporting documents and notifies interested persons of the appeal.	Interested persons notified of appeal.
Within **6 weeks** from the starting date.	Submits 2 copies of any further statement to Inspectorate. This should deal only with issues raised by the questionnaire and any supporting documents.	LPA sends Inspectorate 2 copies of an further statement.	Interested persons send Inspectorate any comments.
Within **9 weeks** from the starting date.	Sends Inspectorate 2 copies of any final comments on the LPA's statement and on any comments made by interested persons. No new evidence is allowed at this stage.	LPA sends Inspectorate 2 copies of final comments on appellant's statement and on any comments made by interested persons. No new evidence is allowed at this stage.	

Normally within **12 weeks** of the starting date, the Planning Inspectorate notifies parties of arrangements for the site visit which may, or may not, be accompanied.

Inspector visits site.

In most cases, within **16 weeks,** the formal decision is received and copied to all parties.

A Guide to Negotiating the Planning Maze

A Guide to Negotiating the Planning Maze

A Guide to Negotiating the Planning Maze